hENGEST

The epic saga of the founding of the
English Nation.

CHRISTOPHER WEBSTER

EK PRESS

PUBLISHED BY EK PRESS

LONDON AND LEEDS

Copyright © Christopher Webster, 2012

ISBN: 978-0-9555753-3-4

A CIP catalogue record for this book is available from the British Library

The cover design uses an image of a reconstruction of the Sutton Hoo helmet, courtesy of Wikipedia Commons, on a parchment background, courtesy of www.myfreetextures.com

Set in Gentium as it is one of the few fonts to include the character 'yogh' (ȝ) which is necessary for most Middle English texts.

DEDICATION

This book is dedicated to my mother, Joyce, who for many years ran the Conisbrough Local History Society and encouraged my early interest in history.

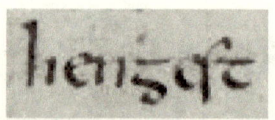

The name "Hengest" as it appears in the handwriting of
Scribe I in the Beowulf MS, fitt XVI, line 1127.

CONTENTS

·INTRODUCTION·

A lost English saga in which the deeds of Hengest and
his followers were preserved for later generations.
—R. M. WILSON[1]

A LOST SAGA?

Stories of kings and other national heroes abound: King
Arthur, Alfred the Great, Hereward the Wake, Robin Hood –
the list is endless. But where are the stories of Hengest, the
founder of the English nation? Most recent history books
dismiss him as a semi-legendary figure, but legendary status
has not stood in the way of *Beowulf*'s popularity. Hengest's
story is as exciting as Beowulf's, and he is a similar figure – a
heroic Germanic warrior. Hengest takes part in several
titanic conflicts, usually winning, but, like Beowulf, losing in
the end in a stirring single combat with Earl Aldolf. There is
the dramatic skullduggery of the Night of the Long Knives,
feasting, betrayal, magic spells, and even a couple of
dragons, though they cannot match the magnificence of the
dragon in *Beowulf*. And the story of Hengest has something
that *Beowulf* lacks - a leading lady. Robert Zemeckis, director
of the recent film *Beowulf* (2007), had to remedy this lack by
making Grendel's mother a shapeshifter, which allowed her
to change from a monster into Angelina Jolie! But the story
of Hengest has its own femme fatale in Rowena, Hengest's
daughter, who lures king Vortigern into marriage, and later
seduces his son, Vortimer, as part of a plot to bring about his
destruction. To add to the magic of the story of Hengest, it is
a kind of prequel to the Arthurian age, featuring well-

known characters like Uther Pendragon and Merlin. The fate of the Hengest story as compared to the Arthur story is eloquently expressed in the introduction to Aurner's *Hengest: A Study In Early English Hero Legend*[2].

> In the inherited traditions of the English race the figure of Saxon Hengest stands second only to that of British Arthur, but the fates of the two in literature have been very different. Everyone recognizes the importance of the legends that have gathered about the person of Arthur, while very little apparent consideration is given to the tales that have made the name of Hengest live, although this name has aroused a mental thrill from the first mention of the Anglo-Saxon conquest to the day when Thomas Jefferson, proposing his device for a United States Seal, wrote, "and on the other side Hengist and Horsa, the Saxon chiefs from whom we claim the honor of being descended, and whose political principles and form of government we have assumed."
> —Aurner (op. cit.) p. 7

This study, by the way, is essential reading for the student of Hengest. Of particular value is the Appendix which contains a table comparing and contrasting all the sources in which Hengest is mentioned.

Unfortunately, unlike Beowulf and King Arthur, the story of Hengest lacks a text. It is probable that such a text existed once, a saga about Hengest, similar in style to the Beowulf saga[3]. Only one manuscript of *Beowulf* survived the ravages of the Vikings and Henry VIII, and many similar sagas must have perished in the flames (for example, *Waldere*, of which two fragments survive). That was probably the fate of *The Saga of Hengest*, except possibly for one page, known as *The Finnesburh Fragment*. This fragment was found in 1705 by the antiquarian George Hicks bound up with a collection of homilies in Lambeth Palace library. The underlying story is known from other sources: Hnæf, leader of the Half-Danes, a tribal group in what is now Denmark, is staying in a hall at Finnesburh, visiting his sister, Hildeburh, who, many years ago, had been married to Finn, the Frisian chief, as a "peaceweaver". The Frisians mount a surprise attack in the early hours of the morning. It is at this point that *The Finnesburh Fragment* begins. The following extract shows where Hengest's name first appears, and gives an idea of the high quality of the poetry:

"That is no dawn from the east; no dragon flies;
nor are the horned gables of this hall burning,
but hurrying towards us is a hostile band,
in bright battle-gear, brandishing swords.
So wake up now, my warriors!
Seize your shields, be steadfast in valour,
fight at the front, and fearlessly hold fast!"
Then rose from rest, with ready courage,
many gold-adorned thegns, garbed in armour.
Sigeferth and Eaha, those able warriors,
went to the door and drew their swords;
and to the other entrance went Ordlaf and Guthlaf,
Hengest himself hastily following them.
—*The Finnesburh Fragment*, 10–17, 28–30

That Hengest is the protagonist of this poem is suggested by the phrase "Hengest himself..." ("Hengest sylf") in the above extract. After another eighteen lines describing the battle the fragment ends, but by a lucky coincidence, the story is continued in one of the digressions in *Beowulf*: Hnæf is killed and Hengest takes over as leader. The Danes manage to hold out until a stalemate is reached. Hengest and the Danes are not strong enough to fight their way to freedom, but Finn is unable to overcome the Danish resistance. A truce is agreed. Hengest's terms for submission are that the Danes shall have equal rights with Finn's own followers. The truce is kept until, a year later, Hengest is reminded of his duty to seek revenge for the death of Hnæf:

He did not disdain the world-wide custom
when Hunlafing laid a sword on his knees:
"Battle Flame", the finest of blades.
Its sharp edge was well known to the Frisians,
and so in turn, to war-minded Finn
came the sword-evil... His hall was decorated
with the lives of his people: a tapestry of blood.
—*Beowulf*, 1142–1153

These two passages, which were composed at some time between the middle of the seventh and the end of the tenth century[4], preserve an oral tradition which is much older. Their authenticity is beyond doubt, but can we be sure that the Hengest referred to in these passages is the same as the Hengest of *The Anglo-Saxon Chronicle*; the Hengest of history? Tolkien, in his essay *Finn and Hengest*, sets out the evidence that the Hengest of *The Finnesburh Fragment*, and the Hengest who settled in Britain are one and the same:

1) Hengest is an odd and rare name.
2) Both bearers of this memorable name were con-
temporaries, and adventurers in the same waters.
—J. R. R. Tolkien, *Finn and Hengest* (1982)[5]

The link between these two sources is important in establishing the historicity of the Hengest figure. His twinning with Horsa, and the link with Hengest-Horsa dieties in Germany, has frequently been cited as evidence of his mythological origin:

In what is now Northern Germany and the north-east of the Netherlands, horse head gables, or gable signs adorned with two rampant horse figures, were referred to as "Hengist and Hors" up until the late 19th century. Other founding horse-associated twin brothers are attested among various other Germanic peoples, and appear in other Indo-European cultures. As a result, scholars have theorized a pan-Germanic

mythological origin for Hengist and Horsa, stemming originally from divine twins found in Proto-Indo-European religion.
—*Wikipedia*[6]

However, the Hengest of *The Finnesburh Fragment* is a flesh and blood hero who fights with heroes whose existence is attested in the poem *Widsith*, among them, Finn Folcwalding and Hnæf Hocing. If Tolkien is right that the Hengest of the fragment is the Hengest of *The Anglo-Saxon Chronicle*, then Hengest is a historical figure. The same cannot be said of his brother, Horsa, who is not mentioned in the earliest sources, and is a shadowy figure at best, whose only claim to fame is his single combat with Katiger in the *Brut*.

OTHER EARLY SOURCES

Another early source provides a link between the Hengest mentioned in *The Finnesburh Fragment* and *Beowulf* and the Hengest of history. Nennius' *Historia Britonum*, written in the early 9th century, is a compilation of much earlier sources. One of them, known as the *Kentish Chronicle*, contains this interesting statement:

> Then came three keels, driven into exile from Germany. In them were the brothers Horsa and Hengest, sons of Wichtgils, son of Witta, son of Wechta, son of Woden, son of Frealaf, son of Fredulf, son of Finn Folcwald, son of Geta.
> —Nennius, *Historia Brittonum* (c. 830) ch. 31

Hengest's genealogy in *The Anglo-Saxon Chronicle* ends with Woden, the logical place, since this is similar to the geneaologies of many other Anglo-Saxon royal families which claim descent from the Anglo-Saxon chief god. The genealogy given by Nennius adds more names including "Finn Folcwald", which is the full name of the king of the

Frisians, as given in *Beowulf* – a clear link between the two sources. Could it be that Hengest was exiled for his part in the Frisian feud? In avenging Hnæf, he broke the terms of the peace treaty, and risked bringing the vengeance of the Frisians on his homeland. Was he therefore "driven into exile" to prevent this happening? This is the interpretation of events that I have used in my reconstruction.

Hengest's arrival in Britain is well documented. It is described in Bede's *Ecclesiastical History* (c. 731) and *The Anglo-Saxon Chronicle* (late 9th century), but the earliest reference to the Anglo-Saxon invaders is Gildas' *Liber Querulus de Excidio et Conquestu Brittanniae* written in the 540's. Gildas does not refer to Hengest by name, but gives several details which agree with later sources:

> At that time all members of the assembly, along with the arrogant usurper Vortigern, are blinded; such is the protection they find for their country (it was, in fact, its destruction) that those wild Saxons, of accursed name, hated by God and men, should be admitted into the island, like wolves into folds, in order to repel the northern nations.
>
> —Gildas, *De Excidio et Conquestu Britanniae* (c. 540) ch. 23

Nennius's *Historia Britonum*, Bede's *Ecclesiastical History* and *The Anglo-Saxon Chronicle* give us the names of the leaders of the Saxons: Hengest and his brother Horsa. The date of this landing (rather than 1066) is probably the most important date in English history, so it is a pity that we can't be sure about it. The traditional date, given by Bede in his *Ecclesiastical History* and by *The Anglo-Saxon Chronicle*, is 449; though Nennius' statement that "the English came to Britain in the consulship of Felix and Taurus" would give a date of 428. This date is supported by archaeological evidence which suggests that the earliest English settlements took place between 420 and 430. It is further confirmed by a reference in Layamon's *Brut* to the visit of St Germanus to Britain:

[Vortimer] sent letters to Rome to Pope Romain,
who sent two bishops, both holy men;
Germain of Auxerre and Louis of Troyes. (p. 49)

We know from hagiography written by Constantius of
Lyon around 480 that St Germain (or Germanus in the Latin
form) visited Britain in 429 with Bishop Lupus of Troyes to
suppress the Pelagian heresy – the belief that man could
save himself by his own free will (a belief that seems to have
been associated with the Celtic church). Since Hengest had
already been in Britain for some time before Vortimer's
reign, a date around 428 seems likely. All the early sources
agree that Hengest was invited to Britain by Vortigern to
help him fight against the Picts; the "Painted People" who
lived to the north of Hadrian's wall:

King Vortigern gave them land in the South-East on
condition that they fought against the Picts. They
fought against the Picts and had victory wherever
they came.
—*The Anglo-Saxon Chronicle*, Anno 449

This was Vortigern's solution to a problem that had
worsened since the Romans withdrew their legions from
Britain in 410. The Picts had crossed Hadrian's wall and were
raiding further and further south. We know from *The Anglo-
Saxon Chronicle* that a final plea for help from Rome was
made in 443, but the Romans were too busy defending
themselves against Attila the Hun. Vortigern's plan, though
successful at first, backfired when Hengest and Horsa turned
against him, as we can see from the entry in *The Anglo-Saxon
Chronicle*:

In this year Hengest and Horsa fought against king
Vortigern at a place called Aegelesthrep, and Horsa
was slain. After that, Hengest and his son, Aesc,
succeeded to the kingdom.
—*The Anglo-Saxon Chronicle*, Anno 449

There are three more short entries recording battles against the Britons, but after that, *The Anglo-Saxon Chronicle* has no more to say about Hengest. Fortunately, Nennius continues Hengest's story in some detail, and though unconfirmed by any of the other early sources, Nennius' reliablity as a source has already been attested by the genealogy which preserves a reference to Hengest's early life, and by his (probably) more accurate dating of Hengest's arrival in Britain. According to Nennius, Vortigern tried to send the Angles away after they had defeated the Picts, but Hengest persuaded Vortigern to allow him to invite even more Angles in return for providing a permanent defence. "Sixteen keels" soon arrived from across the sea bringing hundreds more warriors. They also brought:

> Hengest's daughter, a very beautiful girl. When the keels had arrived, Hengest held a banquet for Vortigern, and his men and he told the girl to serve their drinks. When they were drinking, Satan entered into Vortigern's heart and made him fall in love with her. Through his interpreter he asked her father for her hand, saying "Ask of me what you will, even as much as half my kingdom".
>
> —Nennius, *Historia Brittonum* (c. 830) ch. 37

Hengest asked for Kent and was given it, much to the disgust of the British nobles. Another cause of discontent was the fact that Vortigern, a nominally Christian ruler, had married a heathen. This led to a rebellion of the British nobles against Vortigern, led by his son, Vortimer. Vortimer took power, and fought four battles against the Saxons, eventually driving them out of the country. But when Vortimer died, poisoned by Rowena, Vortigern invited them back again. This time, Hengest was determined to ensure his hold on Britain by tricking the British nobles into attending a peace conference without their weapons. He arranged for his own men to hide their seaxes (the single-edged short swords after which the Saxons were named) and to massacre the Britons at the words; "Nimed eure saxes!" Only Vortigern, at Hengest's command, was spared. Without doubt, the massacre is a blot on Hengest's career, but it must be seen in the context of the times: Barbarossa massacred 3,000 men, and Richard the Lionheart massacred 1,000 prisoners when he was in Cyprus. This ignoble deed is the climax of Hengest's career in Nennius' account. A little later, Hengest's death is mentioned by way of an introduction to the story of King Arthur.

After the massacre, Vortigern fled to a place in Wales, where he tried to build a fortress. Unfortunately the walls kept falling down. He consulted his "twelve wise men" and they recommend a human sacrifice. The boy chosen turned out to be a wizard named Ambrose, who managed to save his life by outwitting Vortigern's wise men when they failed to interpret the meaning of two serpents, one red and one white, which appeared before them. We are now in the realms of magic and prophecy. It is exciting and makes a good story, but is a long way from real history. Despite that, it seems to have captured the imagination of our next chronicler more than anything else in the *Historia Britonum*.

GEOFFREY OF MONMOUTH

Nennius' story of the wizard Ambrose is developed by Geoffrey of Monmouth in his *Historia Regum Britanniae*. This was written in Latin around 1136 and immediately became a best seller. Geoffrey's "history" is a mixture of history, legend and story-telling, though he claimed that he was merely translating "a certain very ancient book written in the British language"[7]. He tells much the same story as Nennius with some changes of detail, for example, he identifies the place as Mount Erith in Wales. But the biggest change is his creation of one of the most memorable of Arthurian characters, Merlin, whom he develops from Nennius' Ambrose, by adding more description, and even more important, a section (Book VII) about his prophecies.

Geoffrey goes on to give us a detailed account of the last

part of Hengest's story. His is the only source for this material, but fortunately, there are a few scraps of other evidence which can be used to cross-check his account. After the Merlin epsiode (which gives away most of the following plot in Merlin's prophecies), Geoffrey describes how Aurelius Ambrosius, the rightful heir to the British throne (Vortigern being a usurper), lands at Totnes in Devon and becomes a focal point for the British resistance. Fortunately, Gildas, our earliest (c. 540) and most reliable source, provides confirmation:

> Their leader was Ambrosius Aurelianus, who was the only Roman who had survived the shock of this storm. Without doubt, his parents, who had worn the purple, were slain in it.
> —Gildas, *De Excidio* (c. 540) ch. 25

Aurelius is said to have brought 3000 Armoricans, (from the part of France now called Brittany) including a contingent of cavalry, and Demetians and Venedotians, soldiers from other parts of Roman empire. He was joined by many Britons and by Picts and Scots. The total, according to Geoffrey, was around 10,000 men. Their first task was to destroy the usurper Vortigern. After destroying Vortigern and his army by setting fire to his castle, Aurelius turned his attention to Hengest, meeting him in battle in a field called Maisbeli. The battle went against Hengest and he retreated to "the castle of Kaerconan, which is now called Cunungeburg"[8]. In the event, Hengest chose not to enter the castle for he realised that it was not strong enough to withstand Aurelius, and he chose to meet him on open ground. There then followed a battle in which Hengest engaged in single combat with his nemesis, Eldol, the Earl of Gloucester, who was seeking revenge for the Saxon massacre at Ambresbury. The victorious earl dragged Hengest through the streets of Conisbrough and then beheaded him. Aurelius, who in contrast to Eldol, "was moderate in all that he did, ordered Hengest to be buried and a barrow of earth to be raised over his body, that being the pagan custom"[9]. After Hengest's death, Aurelius pursued the surviving Anglo-Saxons to York and forced them to surrender. Soon afterwards he died and was succeeded by Uther Pendragon, thus setting the scene for one of the most glorious episodes in British legend, the reign of King Arthur.

Geoffrey's book was the best-seller of the age and was soon translated into the two vernacular languages of the England of those days; Norman French and English. In c. 1150, the Anglo-Norman poet Wace wrote a version of Geoffrey's *Historia* in Norman-French octo-syllable couplets known as the *Roman de Brut*, developing Geoffrey's material, particularly in the Arthurian section, but adding nothing of interest to the Hengest section, except some additional descriptive detail, for example, a description of Hengest's daughter, Rowena.

LAYAMON'S BRUT

Layamon was a little known priest, living at Areley Kings in Worcestershire in the late 12th century. His version of the story of Hengest is contained in his reworking of Wace's *Roman de Brut*, which according to his own introduction, seems to have been his main source, written in about 1190. His material, which differs little from that of Geoffrey and Wace, purports to be a history of Britain from its founding by the legendary Brutus (hence the title, *Brut*) up to the death of Cadwallader, the last Celtic king, the main focus being the story of King Arthur. His work is longer than Geoffrey's or Wace's but most of the additional length results from added descriptive detail rather than new material, which suggests that he was merely embroidering his main source.

The most remarkable thing about Layamon's work is that is written in the Anglo-Saxon alliterative style, which had long since been consigned to the margins of literary activity, and was to die out altogether by the late 14th century (see below for a description of the style). Not only is the style the same, but the language is not far removed from Anglo-Saxon. Indeed, Madden used the term "Semi-Saxon" to describe it. In his introduction he states:

> If we number the words derived from the French (even including some that may have come directly from Latin) we do not find in the earlier text of Layamon's poem so many as fifty.
> —Frederic Madden (ed.) *Layamon's Brut*. London (1847) p. xxii

To give a few examples, *beorn* (warrior) is used many times in Beowulf, three times in Layamon's Hengest section, but not once by Chaucer; *cniht* is the Old English form of the word *knight* which by Chaucer's time had become *knyghte*; *sweord* is also an Old English form; Chaucer uses the form *swerd*. Furthermore, as Le Saux[10] points out: "of Layamon's 411 compounds, 183 are found in both Old English poetry and prose". Layamon's poetry also resembles Anglo-Saxon poetry in style as Madden points out in his introduction to his edition of the Brut:

> It is a remarkable circumstance, that we find preserved in many passages of Layamon's poem the spirit and style of the earlier Anglo-Saxon writers. No one can read his descriptions of battles and scenes of strife, without being reminded of the Ode on Æthelstan's victory at Brunanburh... many phrases are purely Anglo-Saxon.
> —Frederic Madden (ed.) *Layamon's Brut*, (1847) xxiii

It also reveals deep knowledge of English culture and customs, for example, the detailed explanation of the Anglo-Saxon version of the Nordic gods and how they gave their names to the days of the week (see page 18-19), and the welcome ceremony in which the hostess passes the drinking cup to the guests. This ceremony is performed twice by Rowena in the Hengest section (first for Vortigern and secondly for Vortimer) and the custom is explained in detail by the interpreter Keredic (see pp. 27-28). This exactly parallels the scene in *Beowulf* in which Wealhtheow, Hrothgar's queen, welcomes Beowulf (see epigraph on page 26, and the note on page 119). Two briefer descriptions of this ceremony are given in *Beowulf*, lines 1981-1983, where Hygd, Hygelac's wife, takes round the cup, and in lines 2020-2023, where the honours are done by Freawaru, Hrothgar's daughter.

There is also an acute awareness of the language difficulties encountered when the Anglo-Saxons encountered the Romano-British. This is dealt with in the welcome ceremonies described above, but most tellingly in the Night of the Long Knives (see pp. 44-47) when Hengest gives the signal to attack the Britons in the English language, which in the Semi-Saxon of Layamon is: "Nimeð eoure sexes!" ("Take your swords!" – see the note on page 127) knowing that the Britons' failure to understand these words would give them the advantage of surprise.

Finally, Layamon makes numerous mentions of hustings, what Madden calls "the memory of the witengemot", to decide on important matters such as the election of a king (see page 33) and the punishment of Hengest (see page 69). This can be contrasted with the autocratic decision-making process described by Wace. Of course, there are also significant differences between Layamon's style and the style of the heroic poetry of the Anglo-Saxon age, the most notable being the absence of kennings (compound words with the effect of metaphor, for example "whale-road" for sea) and specialised poetic diction. Missing also are certain literary conventions such as the "beasts of battle" (eagles, wolves, ravens) which appear in almost all descriptions of battle in poems as diverse as *The Finnesburh Fragment*, *Exodus*, *Elene*, *Genesis*, *Brunanburh* and *Maldon*. The metre, though still based on the four-stress alliterative line, is also different in some respects (see below). However, taken as a whole, the similarities with classical Anglo-Saxon heroic poetry are much greater than the differences.

ORAL-FORMULAIC POETRY

So is Layamon's Hengest section the text that we have been
looking for? It is far from being the original *Saga of Hengest*,
and it undoubtedly omits much material that the original
contains, as well as adding extraneous material which we
would be unlikely to find in the original, for example the
lengthy section about Merlin which seems to have Celtic
origins. However, sagas like *Beowulf* were not fixed in form.
It is believed that they were originally the result of "oral-
formulaic" improvisation which allowed the "scop" (court
poet) to reshape his material for different audiences in the
way that Hrothgar's scop reshapes the legend of Sigemund
the Dragon-slayer to "sing Beowulf's praise" (line 872). The
use of oral formulas worked on two levels. The first level is
the level of the phrase (see Francis Peabody Magoun's work
on formulaic variation in Old English poetry[11]). The
following is an example from *Beowulf*:

Hroðgar maðelode helm Scildinga (371)
Hrothgar spoke, protector of the Scyldings
Beowulf maðelode bearn Ecgþeowes (529)
Beowulf spoke, son of Ecgtheow

The second level of oral formula is the level of the scene.
In his article on Germanic oral-formulaic poetry, Andersson
lists ten stock scenes of Germanic heroic poetry[12]:

1. Battle scenes in the open
2. Hall scenes of conviviality or celebration
3. Hall battles
4. Journeys in quest of heroic confrontation
5. Sentinal scenes
6. Welcoming scenes
7. The use of intermediaries
8. The consultation of the hero with kings or queens
9. Incitations or flytings
10. Leave-taking scenes

To this list can be added "the hero on the beach", another stock scene identified by D. K. Crowne[13]. In the Hengest sources there are many examples of these stock scenes. Some of them can be found in our earliest sources which may be fragments of the original saga. For example, *The Finnesburh Fragment* is a classic example of a hall battle. Most of the others can be found in the later material from Layamon. It is therefore reasonable to assume that the missing scenes of *The Saga of Hengest* may have had a close resemblence to similar scenes that have survived. Thus the seminal moment of English history, Hengest's landing at Ypwinesfleot (Ebbsfleet), may have been narrated with similar language and content to the landing of Beowulf in Denmark, as the latter is the classic example of the "hero on the beach" scene. I have based my reconstruction on this theory, with the result that the landing scene is adapted from the scene in *Beowulf*.

CHRISTIAN INTERPOLATIONS

The surviving *Beowulf* MS was written hundreds years after the original oral composition and contains several alien elements, such as Christian interpolations, and the many "digressions" referring to the forgotten politics of the Germanic tribes; and though it is written in a mainly West Saxon dialect, it contains evidence of several other dialects, particularly Mercian, Anglian and Northumbrian, suggesting a long history of reworking. Seen against this background, our text takes on a new validity. We can imagine an original which was composed orally by a court poet soon after Hengest's death which was passed on orally and adapted to suit different circumstances, one example being the way it was adapted by the *Beowulf* poet, and which was eventually written down. Layamon's *Hengest* can therefore be seen as a legitimate, though late, version of *The Saga of Hengest* embedded in a much longer text, and which, like the text of *Beowulf*, has gone through many changes. The bottom line is that we can enjoy reading the story of

Hengest in a language and literary style that is strongly reminiscent of the Anglo-Saxon saga.

LAYAMON AS LITERATURE

Another important consideration is the value of the *Brut* as literature. *Beowulf* is now recognised as one of the finest works of literature in the English language, but only after a long period in which it was seen as inferior to the classics of the Greek and Roman world. The problem was partly, as Tolkien humorously pointed out, that for the classically-educated scholars of his time, "Doom [was] held as less literary than hamartia"[14], and partly that the story seemed to put "the irrelevances in the centre and the serious things on the outer edges"[15]. In his essay, Tolkien redressed the balance by pointing out the effectiveness of the monsters as symbols:

> The monsters are not an inexplicable blunder of taste; they are essential, fundamentally allied to the under-lying ideas of the poem, which give it its lofty tone and high seriousness.
> —J. R. R Tolkien, *The Monsters and the Critics* (1937) p. 19

Beowulf has a complex structure based on accounts of battles with three monsters through which are woven references to other incidents (the digressions) which illuminate the main themes. Layamon's *Brut*, on the other hand, is a verse chronicle in which one event follows another with little sense of structure except for a breathless race through time. However, certain episodes in the Hengest section stand out, for example the role of Rowena as a femme fatale, the story of the youth called Merlin, Hengest's last battle and his single combat with Aldolf. In the hands of a master storyteller, these episodes would be further developed to explore the inner life of the main characters and to express the main themes, and many of the intervening incidents would be dropped or referred to in passing. However, if the *Brut* is merely a verse chronicle, it is a very fine one, and there are many passages in which choice of language and use of metre are used to enhance description or characterisation. An example is the scene in which Merlin's mother tells Vortigern how Merlin was conceived (see page 100 for an interlinear translation):

> "One night when I slumbered in sweetest sleep
> there came before me the fairest form
> of a knight in armour, arrayed in gold –
> I saw him in dreams when I was deep in sleep –
> He glided before me, glistening with gold.
> Often he kissed me, often caressed me,
> often approached me, and often enjoyed me,
> until I perceived that I was pregnant.
> When my time came round I gave birth to this boy.
> I haven't the faintest idea who his father is,
> nor whether it were evil, or whether God's will.
> I have no more to tell, as I hope for mercy,
> about my son and how he came to be!"
> The nun curtsied to the king and covered her features.

Arthur Wayne Glowka wrote the following critical appreciation of this passage, in which he compares its literary qualities to one of the finest poems in the canon:

> The balanced rhythms, the frequent use of rhyme and assonance, and the surprises of alliteration give the seduction scene preciousness and intensity. The nun, chaste in habit and manner, nevertheless provides an almost titillating description of her experience with the incubus, a description made so by the poetic technique. My impression is that the nun's intensity argues itself as a kind of apology: any maiden would have succumbed to the beautiful golden vision. Layamon's work here rises to the glories of Keats in *The Eve of St. Agnes*.
> —A. W. Glowka, *The Poetics of Layamon's Brut* (1994)[16]

For more of Glowka's analysis, see page 104, and for a critical appreciation of another two passages from the *Brut*, see pages 89 to 110.

Thus we have in the Hengest section of Layamon's *Brut* an almost complete version of the story of Hengest written in a language and style which is very close to that of the surviving Anglo-Saxon sagas. The main problem is that the 2046 lines of this section are buried in the 16,095 lines of a much longer work which, apart from the Arthurian section, is only available in the long-out-of-print Madden edition. It is surprising that the *Brut* is so neglected considering that it was written at about the same time as the *Nibelungenlied* (c. 1180–1210) the three main manuscripts of which are inscribed in UNESCO's Memory of the World Register in recognition of their historical significance; and before most of the highly regarded Icelandic sagas (written down between 1190–1310). The *Brut* is written in the vernacular (unlike the 12th century *Gesta Danorum* of Saxo Grammaticus which is in Latin) and, as shown above, is of high literary quality. Its neglect can only be attributed to the embarrassment of riches in Anglo-Saxon and Middle English literature. This book aims to rescue the Hengest section from that neglect and make it available in a modern verse translation.

MY RECONSTRUCTION AND TRANSLATION

The beginning of Book 1 is based on *Beowulf*, lines 1–55 with additional information from the *Gesta Danorum*, ch. I. This is followed by a genealogy based on that given by Nennius in *Historia Brittonum*, ch. 31. The next section is adapted from *Gautrek's Saga* to explain how Hengest came to take service with the Half-Danes. The last section of Book 1 is based on the Anglo-Saxon lyric *The Wanderer* which gives a powerful description of how an exile like Hengest must have felt. Book 2 begins with 24 lines of linking material followed by my translation of most of *The Finnesburh Fragment*, and its continuation in the Finn episode in *Beowulf*, lines 1071–1159.

Hengest's journey and landing in Britain is adapted from *Beowulf*, lines 210–319. Books 3 to 7, the bulk of the reconstruction, are my translation of lines 6880–8346 of Layamon's *Brut*, with a few minor changes and additions (which are annotated) The ending, describing Hengest's funeral pyre, is based on the ending of *Beowulf*, lines 3156–3182. Extensive examples of the original texts, with literal interlinear translations, can be found on pages 73 to 110.

The early sources for my reconstruction are written in classical Anglo-Saxon metre which, in simple terms, consists of a four-stress line with a central caesura. The two halves of the line are linked by alliteration which can fall on the first or second stress, or both, in the first half-line, and on the first stress of the second half line. Here is an example in modern English (underlining shows stress, bold shows alliteration):

War-clad **w**arriors   **w**orked the oars (p. 13)

Layamon's *Brut* uses basically the same metre, but more loosely, including greater flexibility in the number of stressed and unstressed syllables and the use of alliteration. Rhyme is also used on occasions, as in this example:

tables were **spread**   with meat and **bread** (p. 27)

However, the similarities are much greater than the differences and so the different sections of the reconstruction blend reasonably well. This is necessarily a brief account of the metrical systems used in the sources. For a much more detailed explanation of classical Anglo-Saxon metre, see the introduction to H. D. Chickering's translation of *Beowulf* (1977)[17], and for an excellent analysis of Layamon's metre, see A. W. Glowka, *The Poetics of Layamon's Brut* (1994)[18].

My model for translation was Seamus Heaney's *Beowulf* (1999) as I believe he has struck the best balance between preserving original features of language and style, such as the rhythm, alliteration, diction, the use of kennings, and elliptical syntax, without obscuring the meaning with too many archaisms. Best of all, his translation often achieves the quality of authentic poetry in its own right. Though, no Seamus Heaney, I have tried to achieve a similar thing; using modern language while still trying to stay close to the original. Since the fourteenth century, English poetry has developed as a rhyming medium, and writing alliterative verse is not easy. For this reason I have preferred to omit alliteration occasionally, rather than force it in by using awkward syntax or vocabulary. However, I retained a few archaisms, partly because they were useful for alliteration, and partly because they help to capture the flavour of the original. The most important of these are as follows:

Angelcynn	the Anglo-Saxons, the English
ætheling	nobleman
bale	evil, especially as an active force
baron	nobleman, useful because it resembles the word "beorn" (warrior) in Anglo-Saxon
brand	sword
burh	fortified place
byrnie	mail shirt
carl	warrior
ferdmen	army, from Anglo-Saxon "fyrd", the citizen army
mickle	big
seax	the Anglo-Saxon single-edged short sword
swain	attendant, squire, or commoner
thegn	a nobleman of the rank below eorl

I have tried to give some shape to the material by dividing it into seven books (see Contents) and by adding an introduction and conclusion (based on *Beowulf*). As I worked on the translation I also noticed that there is a rudimentary Aristotelian structure in Hengest's story. When he arrives in Britain his epithet is "fairest", despite that fact that both Vortigern and the author (Layamon) deplore his heathenism. However, after the Night of the Long Knives in which he kills most of the British nobles by a deceitful trick, his epithets become "treacherous" and "wickedest". This is his harmatia (fatal flaw), one form of which is an error in judgement. This evil act so outrages Aldolf that he becomes obsessed with revenge, thus introducing the element of Nemesis, or in Nordic terms "scathe" (the word is related to the name of the Nordic goddess of revenge, Scaði). The tragic consequences of revenge are introduced in the Finn episode which begins with Finn seeking revenge on the Half-Danes and ends with Hengest taking revenge on Finn. This incident is referred to in *Beowulf* for the same reason. It is sung as a lay by Hrothgar's scop to celebrate Beowulf's victory over Grendel, but contains the hint that somebody might come seeking revenge, thus preparing for the Grendel's mother episode. Revenge is also being sought by Aurelius for the killing of his brother Constans by Vortigern. All these forces combine to bring about Hengest's doom. Like a true Aristotelian hero, Hengest pays for his hamartia with his death, a fact which Aurelius recognises when he stops Aldolf from pursuing his revenge on Hengest's dead body and allows him to be buried with honour according to the custom of his people – a *Beowulf*-style cremation followed by interment in a Sutton Hoo-style burial tumulus.

This book is a by-product of a bigger project which began around ten years ago – to write a *Lord of the Rings*-sized trilogy entitled *The Saga of Hengest*. That ground to a halt through lack of information, so I began a period of research and study which included interlinear translations of the main sources. I am now armed with the information I need and can return to the main project – the novelisation (to borrow a term from Hollywood) of the story of Hengest, now provisionally entitled *English Dawn*. Watch out for it – probably in another ten years time! In the meantime, I hope you enjoy this version.

Christopher Webster, Mol, Belgium, 2010 (revised 2012).

I, SCYLD

Hwæt! We Gardena   in geardagum,
þeodcyninga,   þrym gefrunon,
hu ða æþelingas   ellen fremedon.
Oft Scyld Scefing   sceaþena þreatum,
monegum mægþum,   meodosetla ofteah,
egsode eorlas.
—*BEOWULF*[1]

LISTEN!

We have heard of the ancestors of Anglecynn[2],

how in the dark days when the land lacked a king,

a boat came ashore in Scedeland[3],

and in the boat a boy was found

with swords and shields and a sheaf of corn,

so they named him Scyld, the son of Scef[4].

The people guessed he was sent by god

so they held a council and proclaimed him king.

   He waxed in honour under the world-candle,

won every battle and siezed war-trophies.

Before long all the bordering nations

beyond the whale-road had to give way to him

and pay tribute in gold – he was a good king!

   Later, three sons were born: Beaw, Dan and Angul[5].

From Beaw sprang the tribe of the Geats,
and from Dan the tribe of the Danes.
Angul was the founder of the land of Angeln[6]
which he named after himself – the name still stands.

   Then Scyld departed at the destined time,
still full of strength, to fare to Freya.
His comrades carried him to the sea shore
where a hero's vessel waited in the harbour.
Then they laid down the beloved prince,
the giver of bracelets, in the bottom of the boat,
the mighty one by the mast; many riches were there.
I have never heard of a comelier keel
decked with war-dress, weapons of battle,
bill-blades and byrnies. There lay on his breast
many treasures which he would take with him
over the waves to Woden in Wælhall.
They raised a gleaming standard of gold
high overhead. Their hearts were troubled,
their minds full of mourning. Men cannot say,
nor heroes under heaven, who now has that cargo.

   Then was Angul, beloved king of Angeln,
famed among the folk, his father being departed
to join his ancestors, until to him in turn was born
Godwulf the Great[7]. He ruled graciously
until he was followed by battle-fierce Finn.
Finn fathered Frithuwulf, who begot Frithowald,
who was the father of Woden, named after the god.

Woden begot Wærmund and Wecta.
Wærmund begat Offa[8] – that famous Angle
who gained in his youth the greatest of kingdoms,
and with single sword set the boundary
against his foes at Fifeldore.
Wecta begot Witta, a well-known warrior.
Witta was the father of Wihtgils, who had two sons:
Hengest and Horsa, the heroes of Anglecynn,
who like Angul before them, gave the Angle name
to a new land which was called Britannia before,
and Angleland ever after – despite King Arthur!

Hengest was but a boy when they burned his hall
with his father inside. They were Frisian raiders,
ancient enemies of the Angles and Danes.
Folcwald had not forgotten the festering feud
and sent Sisar to lead a surprise attack.
The gates were torn down, the hall was torched,
and hundreds were slain before Sisar
could be brought to battle by the barons of Angeln.
Wihtgils was burned to death with his wife
as the hall caved in, but Hengest was saved,
with his brother, Horsa, by Herebrand,
who took him, three winters old, across the waves
to a safe haven at Horthaland.
For sixteen summers he grew in strength,
until he was mighty, with muscular arms,

a body heftier than a big brown bear's hulk,
and legs like tree trunks so that he towered
over ordinary men who always looked up to him.

He was taught to fight by a gnarled old ferdman
who showed him the way of the shield and the spear,
the blade and the bow and the battle-axe.
Hengest excelled in the arts of war.
He had strength to hew a helmet in half
the skill to deflect a well-aimed dart,
and above all, the spirit of a stallion,
true to his name, Hengest (the Horse),
free, proud and strong – a stallion indeed!

Then Hengest gathered a host around him,
His brother, Horsa, and Hildegrim,
Oslaf and Guthlaf, Guthere and Eaha,
Harold and Hrotti, Herebrand's sons,
Ulf and Alfhere, Aschere and Oswine;
thirteen of them, brave young thegns –
a hardier host could hardly be found!
That host made a vow – vengeance on Frisia –
ignoring the wisdom of the Witangemot[9]
who advised diplomacy in dealings with Folcwald.

They secretly slipped a ship from its moorings
and fared to Frisia with fierce intent.
They landed and hurried to Folcwald's hall,
shattered its gates, and shook its door posts.
Inside stood sixty stalwart warriors,

but the thirteen thegns were in no way daunted.
They hewed at helmets and hacked off heads,
tore through byrnies and battered shieldsboards.

   Hengest hacked his way through the hall
until at last he found King Folcwald.
Horsa and Hildegrim took care of his bodyguard
while Hengest himself hewed off his head –
Folcwald had paid for his fulsome deed!
Then Hengest saw the mighty Sisar,
where he fought at the front, felling his friends.
He knew that this veteran of Viking raids,
the finest warrior in all of Frisia,
would be no easy matter for a mere youth.
But Scyld, he remembered, didn't shun the fight
with Herebrod for the hand of Alfhild;
though he was only fifteen he fought and won,
so Hengest decided to dare the deed.
He struck at Sisar and sliced his shield,
but Sisar recovered and swung at Hengest,
hacking his helmet from off his head
and cutting his chin clean through to the teeth.
As Hengest staggered, another stroke
from Sisar's sword went through his side.
Then Hengest wrathfully raised his sword
for a stroke with all of his far-famed strength
which ripped Sisar's ring-mail and reamed his belly
so that all his guts spilled onto the ground.

Hengest dispatched him with a dagger in the neck.
Revenge achieved, Hengest ordered retreat
before the Frisian ferdmen arrived.

Those were doughty deeds deserving fame,
but it turned out otherwise by Woden's doom,
and a nithing's name and unnumbered woes
were Hengest's reward for his just revenge.
He was no longer welcome in Horthaland,
and the Anglian people were not pleased to see him,
for Frisia was strong and they feared reprisal.

On wilding ways he wandered thereafter,
bereft of rings and robbed of honour;
friendless, leaderless, forlorn in mind,
weary with sailing on icy seas.
Sometime he spoke his thoughts to the sea-birds:
"I am exiled from Angeln[10],
my native land, and my noble kinsmen,
and now in woe and wintry care
I sail the salt seas, hoping to find
the hall of a king who will give me a home.
Sometimes I dream about the old days,
the lord's retainers receiving treasure,
the harp and the hawk, the horse and the hound,
but I wake again and see wind-blown waves,
the white snow falling and the sea-birds wheeling,
and then the hurt in my heart is heavier

as the memory of happiness melts away.
Where is the treasure-giver; the twisted gold?
Where is the harp? Where are the hall-joys?
Alas the bright cup, the burnished blade!
Alas the for the fame I won in Frisia!
Time has banished it; blanked it out.
Everything in Middle Earth is full of misery;
Wyrd is wearisome, Destiny is doom-laden,
Victory is hollow, happiness is empty,
woman is fickle, life is fleeting."

   Then he thought of Scyld alone in his ship
and remembered how he was rewarded afterwards,
and his hope lifted. Soon he saw land,
the land of the Half-Danes, where Hoc was king,
an ally of the Angles and an enemy of Frisia.
Hoc gave a warm welcome to any warrior,
nithing or not, as he needed men
to fight in his feud against the Frisians,
and the self-same act which had exiled Hengest
earned praise from Hoc and a place in his hall.

2. FiNN

"Ac onwacnigeað nu,   wigend mine,
habbað eowre linda,   hicgeaþ on ellen,
winnað on orde,   wesað onmode!"
ða aras mænig goldhladen ðegn, gyrde hine his swurde.
ða to dura eodon   drihtlice cempan,
Sigeferð and Eaha,   hyra sword getugon,
and æt oþrum durum   Ordlaf and Guþlaf,
and Hengest sylf   hwearf him on laste...
—THE FINNESBURH FRAGMENT[1]

HOC was a good king, a giver of bracelets,

who richly rewarded the rushes of battle.

He was not like Heremod[2] who never rewarded

the Danes with jewels, but left them joyless.

After the fighting in Frisia ended

(they feuded with the Danes as well as the Angles)

he rewarded Hengest with an heirloom blade

and gifts of land. Then he married Gytha,

and soon after that his son was born.

They called him Octa (he became king of Kent).

Octa was followed by a female child,

his darling daughter, the delightful Rowena.

She grew up with Hildeburh, King Hoc's daughter,

until she was sent with silver and gold

as a peaceweaver to Finnesburh, to be partnered to Finn.
He was king of the Frisians, of far-famed lineage;
the son of Folcwald, who was the son of Freawine.
She bore Finn a son and the feud was forgotten
for many happy years.

                    Then Hoc sent Prince Hnæf,
with Hengest to help him, and a troop of Half-Danes.
to visit King Finn in the land of Frisia,
and Hildeburh, who was Hnæf's sister,
and renew their friendship at the Feast of Yule.
Hnæf and Hengest and the Half-Danes were honoured,
given their own hall and a heroes' welcome.

   That night they slept deeply, dreaming of hall-joys,
Till they were awoken by a warning from Hnæf[3],
"That is no dawn from the east; no dragon flies;
nor are the horned gables of this hall burning,
but hurrying towards us is a hostile band,
in bright battle-gear, brandishing swords.
So wake up now, my Half-Dane warriors!
Seize your shields, be steadfast in valour!
Fight at the front, and fearlessly hold fast!"

   Then rose from rest, with ready courage,
many gold-adorned thegns, garbed in armour.
Sigeferth and Eaha, those able warriors,
went to the door, and drew their swords;
and to the other entrance went Ordlaf and Guthlaf,
Hengest himself hastily following them.

The first of the Frisian foe at the door
was battle-young Garulf, though Guthere urged him
not to risk his life in a reckless rush,
but Garulf demanded who held the door.
"My name is Sigeferth, a prince of the Secgan,
a well-known warrior – and I'm waiting for you!"

   Then a deadly battle began in the hall;
shields were hacked in the heroes' hands;
the boar-helms burst, and the burg-floor boomed,
until Garulf fell in the grim fight,
Sisar's[4] son, and good men beside him.
The slain sank to the ground, the raven circled,
swords flashed brightly, byrnies gleamed,
as if the whole of Finnesburh blazed with fire.
I have never heard of worthier heroes,
than those sixty thegns who thanked their lord
for their mead with blood as bondsmen should.

   They fought so fiercely, the Frisians sought a truce,
But many lay dead, deprived of friends:
The Half-Danes' hero, Hnæf of the Scyldings[5],
was fated to fall in the Frisian slaughter.
Hildeburh's loved ones were lost in the linden-play[6],
her son and brother both bowed to fate,
stricken by spears; she was a sorrowful woman!
None doubted why the daughter of Hoc
bewailed her doom when dawning came.

   The battle had taken its toll on the Frisians,

on Finn's own followers, and few were left
to wield their weapons, or make war on Hengest,
Hnæf's loyal liegeman, now leader in his place.
So Finn offered a pact to the new prince:
that the Danes should have another dwelling,
a hall and high-seat, and half the power
should fall to them in Frisian land;
and at the gift-sharing the son of Folcwald
would favour with rings the folk of Hengest.
The pact of peace they plighted further
on both sides firmly. Finn to Hengest
openly promised, upon his honour,
to govern nobly, so none of his men,
by word or deed would doom the treaty.
Oaths were given and gleaming gold
heaped from the hoard.

                                   Hnæf of the Scyldings,
finest of lords, lay on his funeral pyre.
Everything on the pyre was plain to see:
the bloody byrnies, the boar-crested helmets,
the blades of iron, and many brave barons
slain by the sword; at the slaughter they fell.
Then Hildeburh ordered her dear dead son
to be placed on the bier beside his uncle.
Their bone-houses burned in the blazing fire.
Beside them both the bereaved woman wept,
and the minstrel chanted a mournful lay.

The furious fire, fanned by the wind,
belching black smoke, burned the bodies.
The gashes opened, gushing blood
from bitter feud-bites. The fire swallowed up
the flower of both folk in its fierce flames.

   Then hastened those heroes to their new home;
to the high hall in the burh. Hengest still,
through the death-dyed winter, dwelt with Finn,
holding the pact, yet home was in his heart,
though he was powerless to set his ship's prow
over the waters, now winter locked them
in icy fetters.

                        Then another spring
came to the courtyards. The cold days
of winter were gone, the glorious weather
gave life to the land, and longing to Hengest.
The unwilling guest would gladly have gone,
but Hunlafing laid Battle-Flame[7] in his lap,
Hnæf's sword, an heirloom well-known
to the Frisians, and famed in battle.
The sword reminded him that revenge should be taken.
So Hengest, heavy-hearted, hailed his hall-troop,
and like Grendel's mother from the mere returning[8]
to avenge her son, attacked Finn's hall.
Battle-Flame flashed, the burh was reddened
with the blood of foes, and Finn was slain,
but Hildeburh was rescued to return with Hengest.

The Scylding warriors took to their ship
all the chattels the chieftain owned;
whatever they found in Finn's domain
of gems and jewels. The gentle wife,
over the whale's-riding they returned to the Danes.
But cowardly Hoc gave no homecoming to Hengest[9]
for fear of the feud that the Frisians might bring,
and he exiled him to escape their vengeance,
while planning to purchase peace with his gold-hoard.
So Hengest again suffered grim heart-sorrow,
and dwelt for a winter in the wastes of exile,
till he heard of a king who was seeking companions
to fight his battles, in a land called Britainnia.
Vortigern was his name, known by few in Denmark.

Hengest and his thegns prepared three ships,
and filled them with the finest of fighting men:
three hundred knights – not counting the shipmen!
Now was his gift-giving generously repaid!
I have never before heard of ships so bedecked
with better war-gear, or weapons of battle,
than set out for Albion seeking adventure,
nor of omens more favourable: the soothsayer foretold
that their kith and kin, in that distant country
would flourish and thrive for three-hundred years[10].

Time passed quickly[11]. They prepared for sea.
Then the three ships sailed from the shore.
War-clad warriors worked the oars

on a willing journey in their well-braced ships.
Over open waters, blown by the wind,
the three foamy-floaters flew like birds
until quite soon, the second day out,
the sleek war-sloops had sailed so far
that the seafaring men sighted land;
silvery sea-cliffs, sandy shores,
and broad headlands.
                              The high-sea crossed,
their travels at an end, the troop of Angles
went over the side, stepped ashore,
and made their boats fast; their battle-gear clanked.
Then they gave thanks to Thunor and Woden
that the sea was calm and had been easily crossed.
    From high on a bastion a British warrior
whose duty it was to watch the approaches,
saw bright shield-bosses borne from the boat
down the gangplank, an army's war-gear.
His mind was afire to find out about them,
so he spurred his steed straight down to the shore,
and brandished his spear, speaking out boldly:
"Who are you men, armoured in mail,
who come sailing upon the sliding sea-road
to the land of Britannia? Long have I held
the sea-watch in season as the king's coast-warden,
that no pirates might pillage the people of Vortigern.
Never have I seen a noble more mighty

or more haughty!" He was speaking of Hengest.
"That warrior in war-weeds – he's no weak retainer!
That noble bearing cannot belie him!
I must know your lineage before I allow you
to stay here any longer. Hurry up with your answer!"

That noblest man gave the answer he wanted;
the leader of the band unlocked his word-hoard:
"We are of the ancestry of Anglecynn.
My father, Wihtgils , was well-known abroad.
My name is Hengest; this is Horsa, my brother.
We come with brave hearts to the land of Britannia
to seek out your lord and serve him as warriors,
if it is true, as we have been told,
that his people are plundered by Pictish raiders[12].
I can offer your king good counsel in warfare
and the carls he needs to conquer his enemy."

The coast-warden answered with careful words:
"I shall send him a signal about your coming
while you wait in the fortress that is not far away.
I shall also order that your ships are protected
against any enemies, invaders or pirates.
I must go back on guard, may God protect you
through all your ventures. You will soon hear from
    Vortigern."

3. VORTIGERN

Tum omnes consiliarii una cum superbo tyranno
Vortigerno caecantur, adinuenintes tale prae-
sidium, immo excidium patriae ut ferocissimi illi
nefandi nominis saxones deo hominibusque inuisi,
quasi in caulas lupi, in insulam ad retundendas
aquilonales gentes intromitterentur.
—DE EXCIDIO, GILDAS[1]

THE news came quickly to Vortigern the king[2],

that strangers had arrived from across the sea

in well-carved war-keels[3], carrying within

three-hundred carls; like kings they were –

the finest fighters that ever fared here!

Vortigern sent to them to say what they wanted.

They answered wisely, as well as they knew,

and said that they wanted to serve the king,

to follow him loyally, and love him as lord.

   Vortigern the king was then in Canterbury,

where with his men he made high revel.

As soon as they met him they made fair greeting,

and offered to help him here in this land

if he would reward them with renown and riches.

Then answered Vortigern, wary of evil:

"In all my life, as long as I've lived,
many days and nights, I've never seen such knights!
I'm happy you've come and hope you'll stay.
But first you must tell me, in truth and honour,
what warriors you are, and where you are from,
and whether you are worthy and willing to serve me."

Then answered the other, the eldest brother:
"Listen to me, and I will make known
what knights we are, and where we are from.
My name is Hengest, this is Horsa, my brother.
We come from Denmark, dearest of lands,
of that same end that is called Angeln.
There is in our land lamentable news:
after fifteen years the folk assembled,
all our countrymen, and drew their lots.
The longest lots had to leave the country,
for there are too many people to be provided for.
The women bear children like wild deer;
every year they bear a child there!
Upon us it fell to find another land
and we cannot return for life or death,
no, not for anything, not even a king,
so we went away. That's why we are here;
to seek under heaven a home and a ring-giver.
Now we have told you the truth about everything."
(But he failed to tell him about the feud[4].)

Then answered Vortigern, wary of evil:

"I believe you, knight, that you are forthright,
but what religion do you believe in?
and which dear god do you adore?"

  Then answered Hengest, of all knights the fairest –
in all of Britain there was no-one so bold!
"Our gods are good whom we love in our mood[5],
and hope in, and hallow with all our might.
The first is called Phoebus, the second, Saturnus.
The third is called Woden, a most worthy god.
The fourth is called Jupiter, who judges all things.
The fifth is called Mercury, the mightiest over us.
The sixth is called Appolin, an all-seeing god.
The seventh is Tervagant, a terrible war god!
We also have a lady who is our love goddess.
She is beautiful and holy and highly honoured.
Her name is Freya, the fairest of goddesses.
But of all the gods to whom we give praise,
Woden was the greatest in our grandfathers' days;
they loved him more than they loved their lives!
He was their ruler, and they revered him.
The fourth day of the week they gave to his worship,
and to Thunor, Thursday, that they might thrive.
To Freya, their lady, they dedicated Friday.
To Saturnus, Saturday, to the sun, Sunday,
to the moon, Monday, to Tidea, Tuesday."
Thus said Hengest, of all knights the fairest.

  Then answered Vortigern, wary of evil:

"Knights, you are dear to me, but this is disaster!
Your beliefs are cursed; you are not Christians,
but believe in the Devil, whom God has damned.
Your gods are heathen and they are all in hell!
But nevertheless, I will make you my knights,
because of the Picts; a people most fearsome,
who raid my land with ravaging armies,
and cause me shame – and mine is the blame!
If you will wreak revenge on their heads,
I will give you land, and gold in your hand."

    Then answered Hengest, of all knights the fairest:
"If Woden wills it, we will do it!
By Saturnus, let it be thus."
Then they vowed fealty to Vortigern the king.
Hengest went first with Horsa beside him,
then the Danish men, daring in battle,
and next there came the carls of Angeln,
Hengest's countrymen, courageous warriors.
They went to the hall, magnificent all,
and better were clothed and better were fed,
Hengest's swains than Vortigern's thegns.
Then Vortigern's court was held in contempt –
The Britons were sorry for such a sight.

It was not long before news of the enemy
was brought to the king by the British barons:
"The Picts are raiding and wreaking havoc!

Throughout your realm they rape and burn,
and the northern lands are nearly conquered!
Do something!" they said, "or we'll all be dead!"
Vortigern wondered about what to do,
and sent within for all his men.
Hengest came, Horsa came, many heroes came:
the Angles came, the Saxons came,
and the Danish knights, who are doughty in fight.
The king saw these men and was merry!

Then came the Picts, painted and horrible[6],
the furious, fiery fiends of the north,
demon destroyers, out of Albany's wilderness,
robbing and ravaging, raping and pillaging,
fearsome foes of Vortigern's people.
But Hengest and all his high-mooded æthelings,
earlmen of Angeln, eager for battle,
marched to the rescue, reckless of danger.
The battle began; brave men struggled,
shield met shaft; swords bit bone.
Fiendishly they fought, the fated fell.[7]
Battle-flame flashed as it had in Frisia.
Byrnies were bloodied, but the bare-chested Picts
wore only warpaint and woad tattoos
designed by druids to defend their bodies,
thus the name, Picts – the 'painted people'.
But Angle blades bit just as sharply,

and linden shields gave better shelter.
Pictish pikes couldn't pierce ringmail,
well-woven war-nets worked by Weland,
so the work was easy for the warriors of Angeln.
When the day was done, the Picts were defeated,
and finally they fled to the Forth and beyond.
Hengest, victorious, went back to King Vortigern,
who rewarded him richly as a ruler should.

It happened when his majesty was making merry,
on a high-day, a holiday for all his court,
that the son of Wihtgils wondered what to do.
He wanted a council with the king in secret;
so he went to the king who courteously welcomed him.
They drank, they dreamed, delight was theirs[8].
Then Hengest said, "Lord, listen to my words:
I want to report a rumour I've heard
if you will consider my words of counsel
and not be angry about what I say."
Vortigern answered as Hengest desired.
Then said Hengest, of all knights the fairest:
"Lord, I have given my all for your glory;
been your worthy man in your wealthy court,
and in every fight, your bravest knight.
But I have often heard these hateful whispers
among your hirelings. They really hate you –
even to the death if they dared to show it!

Often they spy on you, and speak in whispers
of two young æthelings who live in Armorica;
one is called Uther, the other, Ambrosius.
Their brother was Constans who was king of this land,
and they say he was murdered by drunken Picts,
who you encouraged with ambiguous words.
And now the others will revenge their brother,
take your palaces, and kill your people,
and you and your folk fling out of the country.
That's what they say when they sit together,
because the twin brothers are royally born,
of Androein's kin, those excellent Britons,
and that's why your courtiers always condemn you.
But give me heed and I'll counsel your need.
You need many a knight who is good in a fight,
so give me a castle, or a kingly burh,
where I may live to serve you steadfastly.
I'm despised through you, and could soon be dead,
and wherever I fare I'm not free from care,
unless I lie safely surrounded by walls!
If you grant this I'll show my gratitude,
and settle here properly, and send for my wife,
who is a Saxon woman, and very wise,
and my daughter, Rowena, who is most dear to me.
When I have my kinsmen and more of my housecarls,
I can serve you better, believe me, it's true!"

    Then answered Vortigern, wary of evil,

22

"Send messengers soon and send for your wife,
and your relatives too. I'll receive them with joy,
and when they arrive, I'll reward them with riches,
and feed them well, and clothe them worthily,
but I will not give you a castle or burh,
because you believe in the baleful gods
of heathen lore, like your elders' before,
while all my court are followers of Christ."

Then spoke Hengest, of all knights the fairest:
"Everything I do is advised by you.
So now I will send for my wife and kin,
and my daughter, Rowena, who is most dear to me.
and for more brave men, the best of barons.
As for the land, just give me enough
that a bull's hide will span when it is spread out,
far from all folk, in the middle of a field.
Then neither the poor nor the rich of your people
can blame you for giving a burh to a heathen."
Hengest's request seemed harmless enough
so Vortigern agreed and granted the land.

Hengest took leave and hurried forth
and sent a command to his old homeland.
Then he fared through the land in search of a field
to spread the bull's hide of his cunning bargain.
At last he found a field that he liked,
and bought the biggest bull's hide in Britain.
He took it to a man, a master smith,

who stretched the skin with skillful hands,
and grounds his shears[9] as sharp as a sword,
then carefully, cunningly, cut out a thong
that was long and fine, like a thread of twine.
So fine was the thong, it was many leagues long,
enclosing the burh, which Hengest claimed.
Then he ordered a ditch to be dug
and placed for protection a high palisade:
it was a fort that he made, mickle and mighty!
When the fort was done, he found a name for it.
Written in English in the ancient letters,
it was "Þong-chastre", meaning "Fort of the Thong",
but by confusion of letters[10] it later became
"Doncaster" – the name stands today.

   Not far from there is a land called Linnaeus
where there is a burh called in British, Caer Conan[11],
which is the most beautiful burh in Britain.
He liked it well; it was just what he wished for.
From there the Don ran direct to the sea,
and a high hill held the strongest position.
Hengest renamed Caer Conan, "Coningsburh",
in his own language (it became "Conisbrough"),
and ordered a fortress[12] to be fashioned on the hill
with fine stone walls that no foe could force,
and six great bastions to buttress the tower.
Vortigern also gave gifts to Horsa,
and every warrior was well rewarded.

For many a day things stayed that way:
the Picts lacked the courage to come in the country,
no painted pirates dared pillage from the sea,
and if raiders came they were quickly slain.
Thus did Hengest help King Vortigern.

4. ROWENA

...þa cwom Wealhþeo forð
gan under gyldnum beage,   þær þa godan twegen
sæton suhtergefæderan; þa gyt wæs hiera sib ætgædere,
æghwylc oðrum trywe.   Swylce þær Unferþ þyle
æt fotum sæt frean Scyldinga gehwylc hiora his ferhþe treowde,
þæt he hæfde mod micel,   þeah þe he his magum nære
arfæst æt ecga gelacum.   Spræc ða ides Scyldinga:
"Onfoh þissum fulle,   freodrihten min,
sinces brytta!   þu on sælum wes,
goldwine gumena..."
—*BEOWULF*[1]

IN the meantime came Hengest's kin in their ships,

with his wife and his friends, fifteen hundred riders,

and his dearest Rowena[2], his darling daughter,

a golden-haired girl[3] of goddess-like beauty,

like Freya or Venus or Wælcyries in Wælhall.

Like an elf-girl to look at; like a lioness to fight with;

a Saxon vixen who would out-fox Vortigern!

   Now that the burh had the best of all;

his womenfolk as well as his warrior band,

Hengest invited the king to a banquet.

He said he had readied a room for his coming,

and that if he would come he'd be kindly received.

   The time arrived when the king and his courtiers

went into the hall with his knights and all.
Trumpets were sounded, the hall resounded,
tables were spread with meat and bread;
they ate, they drank; delightful was the burh!

When the feasting was done, the plan was begun:
Hengest went to the room where Rowena stayed
and told her to dress with daring and pride.
The clothes that she wore were woven with gold,
beautifully embroidered by the best seamstresses,
and they clung to her body, betraying her curves;
her rounded bosom and her slim, sleek waist.
She bore in her hand a golden bowl
brimming with wine that was wondrously good.
High-born men led her into the hall
before the king – the fairest thing
ever seen in Britain, before or since!

She curtsied with grace and spoke to the king,
and said these words in the speech of Angeln:
"Laverd king, wæs hæil. For þine kime ich æm uæin!"
Which means in the English of England today:
"Lord king, wassail[4]. It is kind of you to come!"
But though the king heard, he couldn't understand
until a knight called Keredic came to the rescue.
He was the best interpreter in all of Britain.
"Listen, lord king, and I will explain
what the lady said, loveliest of women:
It is the custom in the old country,

when old friends meet, make merry and drink,
that friend says to friend with smiling face:
"Dear friend, wassail!" and the other, "Drink hail!"
The one with the cup then drinks it up,
and another full cup is fetched to his friend.
When that cup comes they kiss three times.
These salutations are used in Saxland,
and also in Angeln they are honoured customs."

Vortigern heard this, wary of evil,
and said in British, for he knew no English:
"Maiden Rowena, raise me a toast!"
She finished the wine, and filled the cup,
gave it to the king, and kissed him three times;
and that's how the custom came to this country:
"Wassail" and "Drink hail" – many delight in it!

The beautiful girl sat beside the king.
He looked at her longingly, she was lovelier than life!
Often he kissed her, often caressed her.
With all his will he wanted this maiden.
The Devil was nearby, who is always sly,
and never did good, disturbing his mood;
he mourned too much to make her his wife.
It was a loathsome thing that a Christian king
should love a heathen, to the harm of his people!
He pleaded with Hengest to promise her hand,
who had good reason to grant his request,
and gave him Rowena, most ravishing of woman.

The king set aside the long-suffering Sevira[5],
his only wife under Christian law
(though he also had concubines by Celtic rite,
and many mistresses – and mysterious hints
were heard of Ardora[6], his beautiful daughter).

Since he could not rightfully marry Rowena
and make her his queen under Christian law,
he followed the ways used in heathen days
before Christianity came to these islands,
and married her quickly in Hengest's high hall
without any bishop, without any Bible;
but as a heathen he wed, and took her to bed.
When he was married he gave marvellous gifts:
the City of London and the land of Kent.

The king had three sons, who were noble knights.
The eldest was Vortimer, then Pascent and Katiger,
but now these sons were sad and sorrowful;
they had no advisor now their mother was gone –
she was a goodly wife who led a Christian life,
but Hengest's daughter was a heathen woman!

It was not long, but a little while,
before the king held a great high feast.
He invited Hengest and his heathen friends:
thither came thegns and knights and swains,
but believers in the Bible boycotted the feast,
for the heathens held all the highest places,

and Christian courtiers were contemptibly treated.
   Hengest came to the king with a greeting,
and drank his health with a toast of "Drink hail!"
Then said Hengest, of all knights the fairest
who lived by heathen lore in those days:
"Listen, lord king. Above everything,
you have my daughter, who is most dear to me,
and I am your father among the folk.
Hear my advice, I offer it freely,
for I wish above all to give you good counsel.
Your barons hate you because of me;
you are hated by thegns, by earls and swains,
and they'll attack you with mighty armies.
And so, King Vortigern, if you want vengeance,
and an end to your enemies, send for my son,
whose name is Octa[7], and Ebissa, his wed-brother,
and give them some land at the northern end.
They have mickle might and are strong in fight,
and will bravely defend your northern borders.
Then you can live your life as you like,
with hawks and hounds and high-born lovers,
and need never fret about foreign warriors."
   Then answered Vortigern, wary of evil:
"Send your messengers into Saxland
for your son, Octa, and your Angle friends.
Make sure he knows well that he has to tell
every knight that is good in a fight,

throughout the country, to come to my court."

This heard Hengest, of all knights the fairest,
and he was happier than ever before.
He sent his messengers into Saxland,
and asked for Octa, and his wed-brother Ebissa,
and all of their kin that wanted to come,
and every knight that wanted to fight.
Throughout three kingdoms the messengers went,
recruiting with promises of rich rewards.

They came in a host, like hail that falls,
in a numerous throng in three hundred ships.
Thirty-thousand æthelings came with Octa
and Ebissa arrived with an unnumbered host.
Thereafter they arrived by five and five,
by six, by seven, by ten and eleven;
and thus they came to this fair country,
heathen warriors in Hengest's service,
filling the land with foreign people,
until no-one could tell who was Briton or Saxon,
or could tell apart the pagans and Christians,
for the pagans were everywhere and arrived so quickly.

When the Britons saw so many strangers
they were deeply sorry and sore at heart.
So they went to the king to tell of their woes,
and with sorrowful voices said to him:
"Listen, lord king, and hear our counsel.
You have brought many heathens into Britain,

and forsake God's law for foreign folk.
So we plead with you for the peace of all
that you desert them and drive them out.
If you don't do right, we'll take up the fight
and drive them out and destroy them ourselves,
or will instead will be slain by them.
Otherwise, invaders will inherit this realm
and live here happily for evermore,
but if you, the king, are the only Christian,
they will not let you be lord for long,
unless you worship their wicked idols.
Then when you die in this world's domain,
your heathen soul will go to hell –
a high price to pay for your pagan bride!"

   Then answered Vortigern, wary of evil:
"I will not desert them, by my quick life!
for Hengest is my father and I am his son,
and his daughter, Rowena, is my rightful wife;
I have wedded her, I have bedded her,
and sent for her family and all her folk.
It would be foolish now to forsake my friends
and drive from the land my beloved Rowena!"

   Then answered the Britons, burning with sorrow:
"Now nevermore will we obey your law,
nor come to your court, nor consider you king,
but we will hate you with all our heart,
and will harm your heathen friends if we can!

Let us pray for help to God's Holy Son!"

Forth went the earls, forth went the barons,
forth went the bishops and the book-learned men.
Forth went the thegns, forth went the swains
and the local folk till they came to London.
There was many a mighty man at the meeting,
and the king's three sons all came to speak there:
There was Vortimer, Pascent and Katiger
and many others that came with the brothers.
Everyone had come who loved Christendom.

All these great men took counsel then
and raised up Vortimer, the eldest son,
and a good Christian, to be Britain's king.
The very first thing that he did as king
was to warn Hengest and Horsa his brother
to leave his kingdom as quickly as they could
or he would beat them, blind and hang them,
and his own father would fare the same,
and all the heathens whoever they were.

Then answered Hengest, of all knights the fairest:
"Here we will wait, winter and summer,
and ride and run with the rightful king
and all who vie with Vortigern shall know
the might of the heathen armies of Hengest!"

Vortimer was wise and wary of Hengest,
and sent an order all over the land
that every Christian should come to his court.

He commanded that all who loved Christendom
should hate the heathens with all their hearts
and should bring their heads to him in London,
and have twelve pennies[8] reward for their prowess.

Vortimer, the young, marched out of London,
and Pascent his brother, and Katiger the other,
for they had heard that Hengest was at Epiford[9]
down by the river that is known as Derwent[10].

There battled then sixty-thousand men.
On one side was Vortimer, Pascent and Katiger
and the Christian people who praised the Lord;
on the other side were the soldiers of Vortigern,
Hengest and his brother and many another.
They came together and combated mightily;
blades bit bones and blood flowed everywhere!

Katiger met Horsa in single combat[11]:
Horsa swung wildly at Katiger's helm
which broke from the blow. Blood gushed out.
Katiger reeled but recovered himself
and speared Horsa, and spared him not,
and there he lay dead, deprived of life's day.

Hengest then fled with all his folk,
the Danes and the Angles and Vortigern the king.
They flew forth to Kent, but Vortimer followed.
There at the sea-brim they made a stand;
stern men strove together; the struggle was long.
Five thousand lay dead at the end of the day,

of Vortigern's swains and Hengest's thegns.

Hengest wondered what he might do,
and saw nearby the answer to his needs:
many good ships drawn up to the shore,
and across the sea he saw an island.
The place is called Thanet[12], it was there they hurried;
the Saxon men, they sought the sea,
and sailed to the safety of the island.

Vortimer followed them with various craft
and surrounded the Saxons on every side,
and from his ships shot a rain of arrows.
Hengest suffered, and never so much!
So he took a spear that was long and strong
with a cloak on the end in order to send
a message to the Britons to beg for a truce.
He wanted to parley, to plead for peace,
to concede the victory and send back Vortigern,
trading him as hostage in hope of freedom,
then sail to Saxland without more suffering.

Vortimer halted and honoured the truce,
while Hengest told Vortigern what to do.
Then he went to the land with the flag in his hand,
and while they were speaking the Saxons were leaping
into their ships and unfurling their sails.
They went with the weather across the wild sea
leaving behind their homes and their loved ones,
and Vortigern the king, who despite everything

still loved Rowena and her heathen kin.
Thus Hengest escaped with anguished heart,
and sailed the swan-road till he came to Saxland.

The Britons were feeling brave and bold;
Vortimer the Young was victorious in everything,
while Vortigern his father was almost a vagrant –
no man was so wretched that he did not revile him.
And so he went wandering for five long winters
while his son, King Vortimer, ruled most valiantly.
The people of this land loved him greatly,
for he treated men mildly and taught them God's law.

He sent letters to Rome to Pope Romain[13]
who sent two bishops, both holy men,
Germain of Auxerre and Louis of Troyes[14].
to travel from Rome to the realm of Britannia.
Vortimer was happier than ever before,
and with every knight he went forthright,
on his bare feet towards the bishops,
and warmly welcomed them to the land of Britain.

Now you may hear how good King Vortimer
spoke with Germain, he was joyful to see him!
"Listen to me Father, of these folk I am king.
I am called Vortimer, my brother is Katiger;
Vortigern is our father; false council follows him!
Into our homeland he brought heathen people,
but we put them to flight as our fiercest foes

and hacked them to death by hundreds and thousands,
sending them to sea so they'll never return.
Now we can love the Lord in this land
and comfort God's folk, and give friendly help
to the poorest people that plough the land.
We shall honour the church and chase away heathens.
Every man's rights shall be respected,
and every thrall shall be offered his freedom.
I put you in charge of the church's land,
and forgive all widows their former taxes,
and Britons shall be like brothers and sisters.
Thus in our day we'll destroy Hengest's way,
and the baleful beliefs that he has brought here.
He ruined my father through his daughter Rowena,
whose beauty bewitched him – to the bane of Britain!
I pray you to press him to abandon this pagan
and restore him to righteousness and Christendom."

   Then Germain answered, he was glad of these words:
"I thank my Saviour who succoured mankind
that he sent such mercy to men like you!"
Then with his bishops he went throughout Britain
and corrected Christendom in the uncouth places
where heathendom held out, or worse, that heresy
preached by Pelagius[15] and proscribed by the Pope:
that Adam marred only himself, not mankind;
that children are like Adam before his fall;
that the law of Moses is as good as the gospel,

and man does not rise through Christ's resurrection.
They uprooted this heresy, much hated by Rome.
Germain also admonished Vortigern
for the harm he had caused by marrying a heathen
and other foul deeds such as fornication
with his daughter Ardora[16] who was only thirteen
when she bore him a child, still a child herself;
and for his polygamy, prohibited by God
(for he had many wives under Celtic law),
and most revolting of all, the regicide
of Constans the king who was killed at his word.

    The miserable dastard, dethroned and disgraced,
fled with his guards to Guorthegirnaim[17],
but Germain followed, and for forty nights
prayed for forgiveness of Vortigern's sins.

    Soon thereafter he went back to Rome
and made his report to Pope Romain,
how he had fought the heresy and the heathen.
And for a while things stayed that way.

Now we return to Vortigern, the wretched.
He still loved Rowena, relished her loveliness,
Hengest's daughter, most delicious of damsels,
beautiful to look at – but the bane of Britain!
    Rowena wondered what she might do,
to avenge the Angles and her uncle's death.
She sent swift messengers to Vortimer the king

and magnificent gifts of many kinds,
of silver and gold and well-worked goods.
She asked his leave to come to live there
with Vortigern, his father, and follow his counsel.

    For his father's good, he granted her request
if she agreed to convert to Christendom.
She decided to do what he demanded.
How unfortunate that he was so unaware!
Alas the good man could not fathom her plan!
But who could outguess this guileful woman?

    Forth she went riding to Vortimer the king.
Fair was their meeting; fair was their greeting:
"Hail to you lord king, Britain's darling!
I have come to you to become a Christian
on whatever day you deem most fit!"
Then was the king pleased with everything.
He believed the traitoress was speaking the truth.

    Trumpets were blown, bliss was in the court!
Men brought good beer before the king;
they sat down at the board with great delight.
In the hall they drank, the harp resounded,
and the bard sang a ballad of the olden time;
while wily Rowena went into a storeroom
where she knew she would find the king's best wine.
She brought from the room a golden bowl,
and began to serve it on the high king's bench.
When she saw the right time she offered the wine,

and curtsying coquettishly, said to the king:
"Lord king, wassail, I am waiting for you!"
Listen how this Saxon siren seduced the king!
The king received her favourably – to his evil fate!
Vortimer spoke British and Rowena Saxish.
To him it was a game and he grinned at her speech.
Listen what she did, this dangerous damsel!
In her bosom she bore, beneath her breasts,
a golden phial filled with poison.
The deceitful Rowena drained the bowl,
till she had half done, to Vortimer's doom.
When she saw him smile, she drew out the phial,
put the bowl to her chin, poured the poison in,
then offered the cup most courteously to him.
The king drank the wine and pronounced it fine,
not tasting at first the treacherous poison!
The day drew on; delight was in the court,
for Vortimer saw nothing and suspected nothing –
had not the damsel drunk the same wine?

When night-time came the courtiers departed,
and the wily Rowena went to her room,
and every knight of her guard forthright.
Then she ordered her swains and also her thegns,
that they should hastily saddle their horses
and hurry in silence away from the hall,
and travel to Þongcaster in the dark of night,
then onto Caer Conan and the safely of the castle,

and say to Vortigern that his son would besiege him,
who, betrayed as he was, would believe the lie.

Now Vortimer realised that he was a victim,
and that no healer could save or succour him.
He sent many messengers over his lands
to tell every knight to come forthright.

By the time they arrived he barely lived.
He asked for their peace and he prayed for them all:
"Of all the barons you're the best in the world,
and my doom is decided: that I shall die.
I give you my gold and all my goods,
and all my wealth, your worship is the greater.
Use this wealth to pay for warriors
and seek revenge on every Saxon,
for when I am gone Hengest will come.
So lay my body and in a bier of bronze
at the same sea-strand where the Saxons land.
As soon as they see it they'll sail away,
for they dare not face me, dead or alive!"
In the middle of this speech the good king's spirit
departed his body to doleful cries.

They bound his body and brought him to London
and buried him honourably beside Belyns-gate[18],
but not at the coast as the king had ordered.
Thus lived Vortimer and thus he died:
Britain's darling, betrayed by beauty!

5. ALÐOLF

"Nimeð eoure sexes   sele mine bernes
& ohtliche eou sturieð   & nænne ne sparieð!"
Bruttes þer weoren riche   ah ne cuðe heo noht þa speche
whæt þa Saxisce men   seiden heom bi-tweonen.
Heo breoden ut þa sæxes   alle bihalues,
heo smiten an riht half,   heo smiten an lift half,
biuoren & bihinden,   heo leiden heom to grunde.
—*BRUT*, LAYAMON[1]

WHEN Vortimer the king was dead and buried,

the Britons fell into baleful counsel

and brought back Vortigern out of exile –

that was a rueful thing, to have Vortigern as king!

Vortigern sent messengers to Hengest in Saxland

and bade him to hurry here with his host

and bring to help him a hundred riders:

"Victory will be easy now Vortimer is dead.

You may come in safety, certain of friendship.

It is better not to bring many warriors,

lest British barons be bitter again.

But Hengest assembled an enormous army

so that he had at sea seven hundred ships,

and each ship he filled with three hundred men.

   The word soon came to Vortigern the king

that Hengest had landed at London, on the Thames.
He had often suffered, but never so much,
and the Britons were sorry and saddened at heart,
for they knew no wisdom in the world that could help.

   Hengest was wary, and it was just as well!
He sent his messenger to meet the king
and greeted King Vortigern with words most fair,
saying that he came as a father to his son
with friendship and love, and would live in peace.
Right would be done, and wrong he would shun.
Peace he would have, and peace he would hold.
He would gladly befriend the British people,
and honour the king more than anything.
But out of Saxland, across the sail-road
he had brought a host of heathen men,
the noblest knights from the northern lands.

   Then said Hengest, of all knights the fairest:
"I will bring my barons before the king
on any day decreed by his court,
to give him the chance to choose among them
two hundred knights to help in his wars,
and guard the king in everything.
The ones not chosen shall return to their land
in peace and friendship to the folk of Britain,
and I will remain with the best of men,
to serve him valiantly – Vortigern the king!"

   The people heard what Hengest had promised,

and were glad to hear his gracious words.
and they hoped for peace, plenty and prosperity.
This heard Hengest, of all knights the fairest,
then he was happier than ever before,
for he was privately planning treachery!
Here Hengest became the wickedest of knights;
and so are all who act underhandedly!
Who would have thought that in this world's-realm
Hengest would deceive his daughter's husband?

A day was appointed for the king and his people
to come together in concord and peace
in a field that was fair, not far from Ambresbury[2].
The place was Aelenge, now known as Stonehenge[3].
There Hengest the wolf, by word or by writ,
made known to the king that he would come
with his warriors, weaponless, to welcome the king,
and the king should bring to act as his bodyguard
the wisest barons that were in Britain
wearing their best, but without any weapons,
so that any bad feeling would not lead to blade-hate.
That's what he said, but it's not what he did,
for Hengest the wolf instructed his warriors
to hide a long seax inside their hose.
When the Saxons and Britons came together,
Hengest said, most deceitful of knights:
"Hail lord king. I give you greeting!

If any of your warriors is carrying a weapon,
send it with friendship far away,
and keep the pact of peace we made."
Thus Hengest addressed the host of Britons.

Then answered Vortigern – he was too unwary!
"If any is so wicked that he has a weapon,
he shall lose his hand by his own good brand,
unless he send it away – the sooner the better!"
They obeyed the king and were left empty-handed.

Knights went upwards, knights went downwards.
Each spoke with the other just like his brother,
but when the Britons were bunched with the Saxons,
Hengest shouted, most hateful of knights,
*"Nimeð eoure sexes[4], sele mine bernes
and ochtliche eou sturieð and nænne spariað!"*
That is to say, in the speech of our time:
"Sieze your seaxes, my strong barons,
and boldly bistir you and spare no-one!"

The British were wise, but did not realise
what the Saxish barons said between them
in their Saxon speech, so strange to the Britons.

They drew their seaxes with secret stealth;
they smote on the right side, they smote on the left side,
before and behind – blood was everywhere!
Many of the king's men were killed that day:
four hundred and five – few were left alive!
Then Hengest seized the king by his cloak

and some of his thegns threatened to kill him,
but Hengest defended his father-in-law,
and held him tight throughout the fight.
The Britons fought back without any blades
but fought with sticks or stones or fists.
They made a good fight but many fell,
and many a Briton was bereft of life.

   Then came an earl whose name was Aldolf,
the Earl of Gloucester, and a goodly knight.
He begged a club which a boy was carrying
and started to swing it like a Saxon berserker.
He hammered at heathen heads and bodies;
before and behind he beat them to the ground.
Fifty-three he killed, then rode to safety.
He galloped to Gloucester and called out his guard,
who went out forthright and foraged for food.
They found corn and cattle and carried it back
and stored it safely as siege provisions,
and the gates were guarded day and night.
Aldolf swore a vow of vengeance on Hengest
and from that day on became Hengest's scathe;
battle is one thing, but betrayal another,
and it fuels the fury of the feud-hatred
a hundred times over as Hengest should know
from the feud at Finnesburh and his slaughter of Finn.

   There let it stand while we speak of the king
whom Hengest had saved but the Saxons would kill.

Hengest forthright commanded each knight:
"Do not take his life for my daughter's sake!
He shall keep his life, but give us his lands
if he wants to live, or it will be worse for him!"
Then fetters were fixed to Vortigern's feet,
and wasn't allowed any victuals or visitors
until he had sworn on a saintly relic
that he would hand everything over to Hengest;
all his castles and all his kingdom,
all his burhs and all his boroughs,
and so he did what was ordered by Hengest,
who took in hand this wonderful land.
Kent he kept, and the land of Linnaeus,
and Coningsburh where his castle was,
but he gave his retainers the rest of the country.
The East Saxons named their homeland, Essex[5].
Those in the south called their homeland, Sussex.
And those in the middle – Middlesex of course!
The Angles named their land, East Anglia.
The southern folk called their homeland, Suffolk,
and Norfolk was named after the northern folk.
Thus came about the kingdoms of England.

6. MERLIN

VORTIGERN the king gave up everything,

and he himself flew over the Severn

far into Welsh-land where he made a stand,

and his people with him that now were poor.

But he had hidden a hoard of treasure,

and bid his men ride both far and wide

and use it to muster fighting men

who would win their bread with well-forged weapons.

The Britons heard, the Scots heard,

and they came there as quickly as they could.

From every side, men began to ride;

many a good man for gold and treasure.

When he had assembled sixty-thousand,

he consulted his barons and his builders:

"Give me guidance for my need is great.

48

Where in the wilderness might I work a castle
wherein I might live with my lords in safety
and hold out against the heathen hordes,
until I win back my boroughs and burhs,
and destroy the enemies who ended my kingship?"

Then answered a man who could counsel well:
"Listen, lord king, for I know just the thing.
The Mount of Reir[2] is a ready-made retreat.
It's a rocky fastness, a fortress impregnable,
that you can make stronger with stone and steel;
and dwell there safe from any danger.
You have, I've been told, much silver and gold
to maintain the hirelings you will need to help you,
and so you might live like a lord and a king."

"Let it be known by all my knights,"
Vortigern said, "that I will hurry
to the Mount of Reir and raise a castle."
The king went there with his thegns and swains,
and they starting digging a ditch for protection.
They seized the land and took command
until all West Wales was in Vortigern's hand.

When the ditch was dug and was deep enough,
they began a wall to crown it all,
laying cement and stone together.
Of machines there were plenty; five and twenty.
They worked all day, but it fell down at night!
For seven nights they were served in this way:

each day built a wall; each night saw it fall!
The king was shaken and shocked to see it;
and so were his helpers – they were afraid of Hengest!
Vortigern was sorry and sent for his sages
and wizards and wise men with ancient wisdom.
They cast their lots and conjured with magic,
to find the truth with their terrible craft,
about why it was that a wall so strong
couldn't stay upright for more than a night.
These wizards and wise men went different ways;
some to the heathlands and some to the highways.
For three whole days they did their best,
but they couldn't discover why the wall fell down.

    There came next day a druid named Joram.
He said if they found a fatherless child
and opened his breast and let out the blood,
mixed it with lime, and laid it in the wall,
then the wall would stand to the end of the world.
King Vortigern listened to Joram's prophecy,
and believed it was true, even though it was evil.
So he sent his servants to search the land
wherever they dared, without fear of death,
and on every road listen to rumours,
about where to find a fatherless child.

    These lords went looking all over the land,
and thought it best to go to the west,
and seek the child where Carmarthen now is.

Beside the burh there was a broad highway,
where all the burh-lads had come out to play.
The knights were tired and troubled at heart,
and decided to stay to watch the boys play.
After a while they began to fight,
as is ever the custom when children are playing.
One smacked the other, the other smote back.
The one called Dinabuz cried out in pain:
"Merlin you dastard, what have you done!
You punched me too hard and will pay for it!
I'm a king's son, and you're a commoner,
and what's worse, your mother's a whore[3],
for she hasn't the foggiest who your father is!
Boys like you are a curse on our country,
and so today I condemn you to death!"

   The knights saw this from where they were sitting,
and immediately arose and eagerly asked
about the doings that Dinabuz described.

   There was in Carmarthen a counsellor called Eli,
whom they consulted about the boy:
"We stand on our rights as Vortigern's knights.
Here we have found a strange young fellow
who name is Merlin, and whose background's a mystery.
So have him arrested and sent to the king,
as you wish to live and keep all your limbs!
And also the woman who is his mother.
If you carry this out, the king will reward you,

but if you do not, you'll be driven out,
and this burh will be burned with all its people!"

Eli answered, the Reeve of Carmarthen:
"I know that this land is in Vortigern's hand,
and we are his men, the more is his honour!
We shall do this gladly and give him what he wants."

Forth went Eli and his ealdormen with him,
and found where Merlin and his mates were playing.
They laid hold of Merlin, and Dinabus laughed.
He thought he'd be punished and thrown into prison,
but it was doomed to be otherwise before all was done!

Now Merlin's mother had mysteriously become
a hooded nun in a high minster.
Eli of Carmarthen came to see her
and took her and Merlin to see King Vortigern
who welcomed them all with warmest looks.
He handed Merlin to twelve good men
of his household troop who would hold him safe.

Then Vortigern spoke and said to the nun:
"Good lady please tell, and all will be well.
Where you were born and who begot you?"

Then answered the nun, naming her father:
"He was named Conan, and was king of this land."

The king answered courteously as if she were kin:
"Good lady please tell, and all will be well.
Here is Merlin your boy – who was it begot him?

Who was held as his father among the folk?"
   Then she bowed her head towards her breast,
and sighed and sat silently for a while,
until at last she said to the king:
"My lord, I will tell you a wonderful tale.
My father, the king, cared so much for me
that when I was girl, at the age of fifteen,
I dwelt in a bower with beautiful handmaids.
One night when I slumbered in sweetest sleep
there came before me the fairest form
of a knight in armour, arrayed in gold.
I saw him in dreams when deep in sleep.
He glided before me, glistening with gold.
Often he kissed me, often caressed me,
often approached me, and often enjoyed me,
until I found out that I was with child.
When the time came to be I gave birth to this boy.
but I haven't the faintest idea who his father is,
nor whether it were evil, or whether God's will.
I have no more to say, as I hope for salvation,
about my son and how he came to be."
The nun then curtsied and covered her features.
   The king thought carefully about what to do,
and summoned his councillors, who called on him
to send for Magan, a marvellous man.
He was a wise scholar with many weird skills;
he knew astronomy, and also astrology,

and learned languages; Latin and Greek.
So Magan came to the court of the king
and greeted him graciously with these words:
"May you be hale and hearty, O king!
I have come to serve you; show me your will."
Then answered the king, telling everything
about the boy that the nun had made known.
Then Magan said, "Strange spirits dwell
in the air around us and remain till Doomsday.
Some are benevolent and some are bad.
One kind of spirit often comes among men;
their name is unusual – "Incubi Daemones".
They don't do much harm, but deceive the people.
Many a man they delude in his dreams,
and many a beauty is betrayed this way,
and even young children are cheated sometimes,
and that's how Merlin was begot of his mother."

 Merlin was summoned and said to the king:
"King, I have come because I was captured,
and I want to know: what is the reason
I am brought to the king like a captive in chains?"
 Then said the king with quickest speech:
"You've come here because you are no man's son,
but let me explain the whole adventure:
I began a building with the best of plans
that has taken away too much of my treasure.
Five thousand men work there every day,

with the hardest stone there is to be had,
But what they lay in the course of a day
has tumbled down by the following dawn;
each stone from the other, struck to the ground!
And now my wise men and my wizards say
that if I take blood from out of your breast
and mix it with lime to lay on the stones
then it will stand to the Second Coming.
So now you know what will happen to you."

When Merlin heard, his mood was angry,
and he said these words in a wrathful voice:
"Never will God, in his great mercy,
let your castle be bound with human blood,
nor will your stones ever stand up,
for your so-called wise men are witless fools
to tell such lies – they are deceiving you!
Let Joram your sage show himself,
and all his companions come along with him,
and if I can tell you in truthful words
about your wall and why it falls down,
and prove that their tales cannot be trusted,
give me their heads if I make your wall hold."

Then answered the king with quivering voice:
"Here is my hand, I will hold to this covenant!"

Joram the sage was brought to the king
and seven of his friends (they were fated to die!)
Merlin was grim and spoke thus gravely:

"Tell me you liar and loathsome traitor,
why does this wall weaken and fall,
and in the ditch what will be discovered?"
Joram was still for he could not tell.

Then said Merlin: "Let's make a covenant.
Dig this ditch down seven feet deeper
and you'll find a stone astoundingly beautiful
that is broad and fair for folk to behold."

So the ditch was dug seven feet deeper
and they found straightaway the stone he described.
Then he said to the king: "Hold to the covenant!"
and turned to Joram and said to him:
"Tell me, Joram, most hateful man,
and tell the king, what kind of thing
has taken station under this stone?"
Joram was still for he could not tell.

Then Merlin said: "You will find much water.
Remove this rock and it shall be revealed."

So they moved the stone and there it was,
as he had told the king. Then he continued:
"Tell me Joram, the worst of wizards,
"what dwells in the water, winter and summer?"
Joram was still for he could not tell.
Then he said to the king: "Hold to the covenant!
Cause this water to be carried away
and you will find in the ditch two dreadful dragons,
One on the north side, one on the south side.

They are very unlike: one is milk-white,
and the other blood-red, boldest of worms,
and every night they come out and fight
and because of this wonder your walls keep falling –
because of the dragons, not for lack of my blood!"

   The monarch was happy, and his men too
(but not long afterwards they were feeling sorry!)
When the water was drawn and the ditch was empty,
two dragons came out and made a great din,
and battled dangerously down in the ditch.
Few men had seen a fiercer fight.
Flames of fire flew from their mouths,
their looks were grim as they grappled each other.
The white was above, then he was beneath,
then the red dragon ripped him viciously,
and they hurried away to hide in their holes.

   Vortigern the king saw this marvellous thing
and respected Merlin more than all his mages,
and hated Joram, and sent him to justice,
with all his companions according to his covenant.

   Then he went to his hall taking Merlin with him.
"Merlin you're welcome," he said most winningly.
"I will give you gifts and goods a-plenty;
glittering gold and gleaming jewels."
He wanted his help to win back his land,
but it turned out differently before the day's end!
"Tell me Merlin, my most dear friend,

what do they mean, that unholy din,
and the stone, and the water, and the wondrous fight?
After you've told me, tell me how to act;
and what I must do to win back my kingdom
from hateful Hengest, who has harmed my people."

Then Merlin answered, "You are ill-advised
to ask of the dragons that made the din,
and about the meaning of their mighty combat.
They represent kings that are yet to come,
and their fights and their fears and their fated folk.
But if you were wise and willing to listen,
I'd tell of the cares that are coming to you."

Then Vortigern said, "Speak to me, Merlin,
"of the future, and of the fate that awaits me."

He answered boldly, with blithe tone of voice:
"I will reveal it, but you will rue it! –
King, see to yourself, for sorrow is given
to Constantine's kin! You killed his son,
the noble Constans, who was king in this land,
using the Picts to kill him by proxy!
Then, like a fool, you brought foreign people
to Britain – the Saxons! Therefore you'll suffer!
Now are the barons of Britain arriving;
Aurelius and Uther – now you know it!
They shall land tomorrow, at the port of Totnes[4]
with seven hundred ships sailing from Armorica[5].
Now you have bane besieging both sides:

You have foes before you, and fiends behind you!
So flee away as fast as you can –
though wherever you fly they are sure to follow you.
Ambrosius Aurelius shall inherit this kingdom,
but shall suffer death through a draft of poison.
And afterwards Uther shall rule in his place.
Alas! that brave baron will die in battle.
But before he dies he shall defy his foes.
He shall father a son who'll be famed down the ages,
who shall be a wild boar bristling with steel!
He shall expel all the Angles and Saxons,
and as far as Rome extend his rule.
But his own offspring shall one day betray him
and the white dragon shall slay the red
and ever afterwards rule this country
until the end of the world, which shall come
in the year two-thousand and ninety-one[6]."

7. Aurelius

Wulf Wonreding wæpne geræhte,
þæt him for swenge swat ædrum sprong
forð under fexe. Næs he forht swa ðeh,
gomela Scilfing, ac forgeald hraðe
wyrsan wrixle wælhlem þone,
syððan ðeodcyning þyder oncirde.
Ne meahte se snella sunu Wonredes
ealdum ceorle ondslyht giofan,
ac he him on heafde helm ær gescer,
þæt he blode fah bugan sceolde,
feoll on foldan...
—*BEOWULF*[1]

MEANWHILE from Armorica came Aurelius and Uther

to Dartmouth in Devon, then inland to Totnes.

The Britons were glad to hear this good news,

and came out of the woods and wildernesses

by sixty and by sixty, and by seven hundred,

by thirty and by thirty, and by many thousands.

When they came together it seemed good to them,

for the brothers from Brittany had brought an army

which was bolstered now by many bold Britons;

an enormous army to avenge their wrongs;

the harm that Hengest had heaped upon them,

who had butchered their barons and bishops with seaxes,

and cut to pieces many good people.

They held a meeting with their wisest men
where they took Aurelius, the elder brother,
and appointed him king with loud acclamation.
Then were the Britons filled with bliss,
and those who were mournful before were merry!

The news soon came to Vortigern the king
that Aurelius was appointed king in his place.
He was full of woe – and worse would follow!
So he sought the safety of a secluded castle,
that is called Genoure[2], upon a great mountain,
Cloard is it's name, the land is called Hergin,
near the River Wye, that fair-flowing water.
Vortigern's men filched all that they found;
weapons to fight with and wood to warm them.
They carried as much as they could to the castle,
so that they had enough, though it was little help!

Aurelius and Uther were aware of Vortigern
hiding in Cloard, enclosed in a castle.
Trumpets were blown and their barons assembled;
innumerable folk of numerous lands.
They marched to Genoure where Vortigern waited.
A king was within; a king was without!
Knights fought there with fierce encounters,
and every good man girded himself.

When Aurelius failed to force a victory,
a band of warriors went into the wood,

felled many trees and took them to the castle.
They dragged them in to the castle ditch
then set them alight with flaming torches.
They called to Vortigern, "This will warm you!
For you slew Constans, Constantine's son,
the rightful king, but Aurelius is come,
and Uther his brother, to bring you bale!"

The wind fanned the fire and it flared up fiercely,
and the castle burned – brightly it blazed!
No knight or squire could fight that fire!
It burnt the halls; it burnt the walls,
and Vortigern himself was a hapless victim
as it ate up everything that was trapped inside.
That was the end of the evil Vortigern!

When Aurelius had command of all the land,
he sent for the earl whose name was Aldolf,
Aldolf of Gloucester, the greatest of knights,
and in memory of Ambresbury, made him his steward.

By now Aurelius, and Uther his brother,
had felled their foes and were full of joy.
Hengest heard it, wickedest of knights,
and felt afraid, fiendishly so!
He marched his ferdmen, fleeing to Coningsburh,
in hope he could find a hiding place there.
But Aurelius marched forth and led his folk north,
marching with might by day and by night.

The Britons were bold and braved every danger
because Aurelius had a numerous army.

    The land was ravaged and ruin was everywhere;
the churches burnt and the Britons killed.
Then Aurelius the king, Britain's darling,
said, "If I survive and come back alive,
and it be God's will, who shaped the world,
that in safety I might obtain my right
I'll rebuild the churches throughout all of Britain,
and give to each knight what is fair and right,
and to every man, both old and young,
I will be gracious – if God will grant victory!"

    To Hengest came news of Aurelius the king
that he fielded a force of innumerable folk.
Then said Hengest, most treacherous of knights:
"Listen my men, honour awaits you!
For here comes Aurelius and Uther his brother.
They bring many folk, but all are fated,
for the king is unwise, and so are his knights,
and a knave is his brother, the one as the other.
Therefore may the Britons be much the unbolder:
when the head is bad, the helpers are worse!
Remember these words, which I now say:
better are our fifty then their five hundred,
as they found out when we fought before!
We shall make a stand, drive them from the land,
then rule this realm by right of conquest!"

Thus said Hengest, wickedest of knights,
and emboldened his barons to prepare for battle –
but before the week passed it worked out otherwise!

Soon the news came to noble Aurelius
that Hengest made ready on mount³ nearby.
Aurelius had cavalrymen for companions;
and many bold Britons, who made their boast,
and also Welshmen, wondrous many.
He ordered his knights by day and night,
to wear their weapons as if walking to battle,
and beware of Hengest and his heathen hordes.
　When Hengest heard that the host was near,
he commanded his men to march against them;
the Danish knights who are doughty in battle,
the Saxon earlmen led by Ebissa
and the Angle ferdmen led by Octa.
　When Aurelius was aware that Hengest came there,
he went into the field, sheltered by his shield,
and took forthright ten thousand knights
who were his best and bravest barons.
Ten thousand Welshmen he sent to the wood
Ten thousand Scots he sent to the flank
to harry the heathen on highway and byway.
He held to himself his heavy-armed house-troops;
and set up his shield-wall like a wild wood.
　Then called Aldolf, the earl of Gloucester,

a skilled swordsman who was Hengest's scathe:
"If the Lord should grant, who gives all gifts,
a single combat with that Saxon slaughterer,
who has lived too long in the land of Albion,
and betrayed my friends with bloody seaxes,
I will fight that heathen and hack him to death!
Then shall I say these soothest words:
that God himself has granted victory,
and revenged my kin whom Hengest killed!"

Scarcely was his speech said to the end
when they saw the blond-haired Hengest approaching
with thousands of thegns thronging behind him.
They came together and clashed in battle,
the Draco banner[4] of the Red Dragon,
and the White Dragon of Wihtgils' son,
joining in a bloody battle for survival –
Merlin's prophecy had come to pass!

There stern warriors strove together.
Helms were shattered, knights were battered,
steel struck bone; bane was rife!
In the street ran streams of blood
and the grass changed colour from green to red!

When Hengest saw that his help had failed,
he flew from the fight with fleetest foot,
as did his folk; they followed quickly!

The Christians came after and attacked them again,
and called on Christ to come to their aid,

and the heathen people appealed to their gods:
"O, Tervagant, why do you treat us like this?"
When Hengest saw his host withdraw,
and the Christian men coming on quickly,
he fled through and through to Coningsburh,
and sought for safety inside the fortress.
But King Aurelius came quickly after him
and called to his lords in his loudest voice:
"Run forth and forth; Hengest has gone north!"
and soon they came to Coningsburh.

When Hengest saw this harrying host,
he was most wrath, and said to his warriors:
"I will flee no more, but will fight them here,
with my son, Octa, and Ebissa, his wed-brother!
All my soldiers stir your weapons,
fight them fiercely with fiendish slaughter!
If we fail to fell them it is we who are fated
to lay dead on the field deprived of friends!"

Hengest left the fort and marched to the field
and made a shield-wall with all his warriors,
in front of Aurelius' mighty army.
Then began the biggest battle:
that the land of Britain has seen
since it was founded by Trojan Brutus!
There was many a dint dealt in that combat
and the Christians were well nigh overcome.
But into the fight came five thousand riders

that King Aurelius had placed in reserve.
They charged the heathen and hacked them down.
There was strong fighting, stern combat!

Then came the Earl, Aldolf of Gloucester,
and found Hengest, most hated of knights,
where he fought fiercely, felling Christians.
He lifted his sword and struck at Hengest,
who held up his shield to save his life,
but Aldolf smote the shield in two!
Then Hengest leapt at him, like a lion he was,
and smote his helm so it split in half.
They hewed each other; the wounds were grim.
Steel struck steel and sparked with fire.
Then Aldolf, exhausted, fell to the ground,
but was helped by Gorlois, another great warrior.

Aldolf renewed his attack with eagerness,
and heaved his sword and swung it down
on Hengest's hand so that he dropped his brand.
Then he gripped him quickly, with his grim looks,
by the iron nasal of his Northman's helmet[5]
and with great strength he struck him down,
then brought him up as though he would break him,
and in a strong armlock, led him away.
Now was Hengest beaten by Aldolf, brave man!

Then cried Aldolf, the earl of Gloucester:
"Hengest, it is not so merry as it was in Ambresbury
where you bloodied your blades with British lives!

With sly treachery you slew my kindred.
Now you shall pay for it; part with your friends,
and with fearsome death forsake the world!"
Hengest's hope was gone, for help there was none.

Aldolf led Hengest to Aurelius the king
and greeted him with these gracious words:
"All hail, Aurelius, noble ætheling,
I bring before you the bane of your kindred;
Hengest the heathen whose hordes so harmed us.
God granted my prayer and gave me victory.
Now I give him to you for your good judgement.
Let hirelings' children play with this hound
and shoot toy arrows at him as a target."

Then answered the king with quick, calm voice:
"I thank you, Aldolf, my boldest baron,
you are dear as my life, and loved in my court."

There men took Hengest, and there bound Hengest.
Then was Hengest the most wretched of knights.
His host was harried, and the heathens fled.
When his son, Octa, saw his father's defeat,
he escaped with Ebissa, his brother-in-law,
and hurried to York with harm enough,
where he pulled down halls to repair the walls.
Some of his warriors went to the wood,
where Aurelius' footsoldiers felled them like trees.

Then the king was pleased with everything.
He went into Coningsburh with all his folk,

thanking God for the might which won the fight.
Three days and nights the king dwelt there
to heal the wounds of his weary warriors,
and rest in the burh their weary bones.

When the third day came Aurelius caused
trumpets to sound and summon his earls
to come to a husting to hear his words.
When they had come, the king asked their council.
What did his æthelings advise him to do?
By what death should the heathen die,
and how might he best avenge his friends
who lay dead in Ambresbury deprived of life-day?

Then Ældadus stood up and spoke to the king,
towards God he was good, a gracious bishop,
he was Aldolf's brother (he had no other):
"Lord king, listen to what I say.
I will make a doom how he should die,
for of all men on earth he is the most hateful.
He is a heathen hound and hell is his home.
There he shall suffer for his sin and treachery!
My lord, listen well to the tale I will tell:

A king was in Jerusalem, whose name was Saul,
and in heathendom was another king
who was named Agag[6], who hated Jerusalem.
He was king of the Amalech. Evil was in him;
He hated Jerusalem with harm in his heart.
He would never make peace, but pillaged and raped.

He burnt them and slew them with sorrow enough!
It befell when Agag was sitting in state
that his mood was troubled, so he told his men:
"Hurry to your horses, the host shall ride,
for we are going to attack Jerusalem!"
Then they pillaged the land and laid waste the towns.

When the Israelite leaders who lived in Jerusalem
saw these atrocities they advanced against him,
and fought with him fiercely, and overcame him,
and killed their enemies and captured Agag.
They brought him in chains to Saul the king
who asked the advice of his noblest æthelings,
how he should punish the pagan king.

Then up leapt Samuel, a prophet of Israel,
a most holy man, in the Lord's High Temple;
no man in the land was so learned in God's law.
He made Agag go to the market place
and bade his men bind him to a stake
and in his right hand he took his good brand,
and the good man, Samuel, said these words:
"You are called Agag, and you will receive
my just judgement for destroying Jerusalem.
Because you have harried this holy city
and deprived of life-day many dear friends,
as I hope for mercy, you shall do no more!"
Then he took his sword and sliced him in pieces,
like joints of meat in Jerusalem's market,

and scattered the pieces thoughout the streets.
Thus Samuel did, and thus should you."

    Aldolf heard this, the Earl of Gloucester,
and leapt towards Hengest, like a lion he was,
and grabbed his hair by which he hauled him,
through and through the streets of Coningsburh,
and outside the burh he had him bound.
Then he swung his sword, and smote off his head;

    The noble Aurelius, admired Aldolf's ardour,
but he was a wise and moderate man
and forbade that his body be badly treated:
"Hengest has paid the price of his treachery.
You have the victory, but vengeance is God's;
no disrespect must be shown to the dead."
Then Aurelius offered the Angles his body
to cremate him according to their custom.

They fashioned a funeral pyre, filled it with trophies,
hung it with helmets, hardest of battle-boards,
and the best of byrnies. Their beloved lord
they laid in the middle, then they lit the fire.
The flames crackled like cries of mourning
as they devoured the dear, doomed body.
Later they buried his blackened bones
in a barrow-grave[7] near the gates of his castle.
Then round the barrow twelve barons rode,
mourning for their lord and lamenting his death;

while the wordsmith wove a worthy epitaph,

weighing his worth, and his warlike achievements,

so that in after-days the English would remember him

as their folk-forefather and founder of their nation.

> Cwædon þæt he wære   woruld-cyning
> mannum mildust   and mon-þwærust,
> leodum liðost   and lof-geornost.
> —*BEOWULF*[8]

8 ORiGiNAL TEXTS

Five samples of the original texts are given below with a literal interlinear translation followed by a short critical appreciation. These are: the complete *Finnesburh Fragment*, the complete Finn episode from *Beowulf*, and three extracts from Layamon's *Brut*. To read them you will need to learn the following letters which are not in the modern alphabet.

SYMBOL	NAME	PRONUNCIATION
Æ, æ	*œsh*	'a' as in 'hat'
Þ, þ	*thorn*	'th' as in 'thin'
Ð, ð	*eth*	'th' as in 'then'
3, 3	*yogh*	'y' (/j/) or 'gh' (/x/)

THE FINNESBURH FRAGMENT

The text is a transcript of a manuscript page found by George Hickes in the late 17th century and published in: Hickes, *Linguarum. Veterum Septentrionalium Thesaurus grammatico-criticus et archaeologicus*, vol 2 (Oxford, 1705). Since then the original manuscript has been lost. The text is unique in the corpus of Anglo-Saxon heroic poetry because it lacks Christian references, suggesting an early date of composition. The events described in the fragment probably date from a few years before Hengest's arrival in England in 449 (see pp. vi-viii for a discussion of a possible earlier date).

...[hor]nas byrnað?"

...gables are burning?"

Hnæf hleoþrode ða,   heaþogeong cyning:

Hnæf spoke,   the warlike young king:

"Ne ðis ne dagað eastan,   ne her draca ne fleogeð,

"Neither is this the eastern dawn,   nor is a dragon flying here,

ne her ðisse healle   hornas ne byrnað.

nor of this hall   are the gables burning.

Ac her forþ berað;   fugelas singað, [5]

But here they bear forth;   birds cry,

gylleð græghama,   guðwudu hlynneð,

the grey-coated wolf bays,   war-wood clashes,

scyld scefte oncwyð.   Nu scyneð þes mona,

shield answers shaft.   Now the moon shines,

waðol under wolcnum.   Nu arisað weadæda

wandering under the clouds.   Now woeful deeds will be done

ðe ðisne folces nið   fremman willað.

which this peoples' hatred   desires to fulfil.

Ac onwacnigeað nu,   wigend mine, [10]

But awake now,   my warriors,

habbað eowre linda,   hicgeaþ on ellen,

grasp your linden-wood shields,   be courageous,

winnað on orde,   wesað onmode!"

fight at the front,   be high-spirited!"

ða aras mænig goldhladen ðegn,   gyrde hine his swurde.

Then arose many gold-laden thegns,   girded on his sword.

Ða to dura eodon   drihtlice cempan,

Then moved to the door   the noble champions,

Sigeferð and Eaha,   hyra sword getugon, [15]

Sigeferth and Eaha,   drew their swords,

and æt oþrum durum   Ordlaf and Guþlaf,
and at the other door   Ordlaf and Guthlaf
and Hengest sylf   hwearf him on laste.
and Hengest himself   came just behind them.
Ða gyt Garulf   Guðere styrde
Then Garulf   was exhorted by Guthere
ðæt he swa freolic feorh   forman siþe
that his excellent life   at the first journey
to ðære healle durum,   hyrsta ne bære, [20]
to the doors of the hall,   armoured, he should not risk,
nu hyt niþa heard   anyman wolde,
now that one hard in hatred   wished to take it away,
ac he frægn ofer eal,   undearninga,
but he asked over all,   openly,
deormod hæleþ,   hwa ða duru heolde.
the daring-hearted hero,   who held the door.
"Sigeferþ is min nama," cweþ he,   "ic eom Secgena leod,
"Sigeferth is my name," said he,   "I am a man of the Secgan,
wreccea wide cuð;   fæla ic weana gebad, [25]
an adventurer widely known;   I have endured many misfortunes,
heardra hilda,   ðe is gyt her witod
fierce battles,   even now appointed here for you
swæþer ðu sylf to me   secean wylle!"
which for yourself   you will attain!"
Ða wæs on healle   wælslihta gehlyn;
Then was in the hall   the tumult of carnage,
sceolde cellod bord   cenum on handa,
the round shield-board   in the hands of the bold,

banhelm berstan   buruhðelu dynede, [30]

the bone-helm burst,   the boards of the burg resounded,

oð æt ðære guðe,   Garulf gecrang,

until in the battle,   Garulf fell,

ealra ærest   eorðbuendra,

the first of all   of the dwellers in the land,

Guðlafes sunu,   ymbe hyne godra fæla

Guthlaf's son,   around him many good

hwearflicra hræw.   Hræfen wandrode,

mortals' carcases.   The raven hovered,

sweart and sealobrun.   Swurdleoma stod, [35]

dusky and dark-brown.   Sword-light stood,

swylce eal Finnsburuh   fyrenu wære.

as if all of Finnesburh   were in flames.

Ne gefrægn ic næfre wurþlicor,   æt wera hilde,

I have never heard, more worthily,   in battle of men,

sixtig sigebeorna   sel gebæran,

of sixty victory-warriors   bearing themselves better,

ne nefre swetne medo   sel forgyldan

nor ever for sweet mead   making better requital

ðonne Hnæfe guldan   his hægstealdas. [40]

than to Hnaef gave   his retainers.

Hig fuhton fif dagas,   swa hyra nan ne feol

They fought for five days,   as none of them fell,

drihtgesiða,   ac hig ða duru heoldon.

the troop-companions,   but they held the doors.

Ða gewat him wund hæleð   on wæg gangan.

Then the hero went wounded,   passing away.

sæde þæt his byrne   abrocen wære, [45]

He said that his byrnie   was broken apart,

heresceorp unhror,   and eac wæs his helm ðyrel.

his war-shirt weak,   and also his helmet was pierced.

Ða hine sona frægn   folces hyrde,

Then immediately asked him   the protector of the people,

hu ða wigend hyra   wunda genæson,

how well the warriors their   wounds survived,

oððe hwæþer ðæra hyssa...

or which of the young men....

When we read the these words we are face to face with the original *Saga of Hengest* – in the sense of a version of the saga composed in the Anglo-Saxon period, probably earlier than *Beowulf* because of its lack of Christian references (see above). It is true that Tolkien in *Finn and Hengest* (1982) described this fragment as part of a lay (a shorter heroic poem dealing with one incident) and this seems to be confirmed by the *Beowulf* poet himself who refers to it as a "leoð" ("lay", see page 87). However, we know that lays were often combined into longer narratives. Indeed, *Beowulf* itself is said to comprise several lays which have been welded together (see Owen-Crocker, 2000). However, it may be that *The Finnesburh Fragment* is not a lay at all, but part of a much bigger work. The phrase "Hengest sylf" suggests that the main focus of the text is not the Finnesburh feud, but Hengest. This episode marks the point at which Hengest comes to the fore, shows his leadership, and deals with the dilemma of whether or not to take revenge for Prince Hnaef. Whether the version in *The Finnesburh Fragment* is a lay or not is in any case immaterial. Anglo-Saxon poetry in the heroic age was oral, and the stories and language were recycled and reused in many different forms (see the discussion of oral-formulaic poetry on pp. xiv-xv). The important point is that the story of the Finnesburh feud is a seminal episode in the life of Hengest and would, no doubt, have appeared in some form in the full saga. It is significant that, despite the scant amount of Anglo-Saxon heroic poetry that has survived, Hengest makes an appearance in the two finest examples, suggesting that, though his full saga is lost, he was a key figure in Anglo-Saxon heroic literature.

The Finnesburh fragment, apart from giving us a idea of the content of original Saga of Hengest, also gives us a taste of its poetic quality. Most critics, even Tolkien, who was among the first to make a plea for *Beowulf* on its merits as literature, have approached *The Finnesburh Fragment* in the spirit of a jigsaw-puzzle. But now that the puzzle has been pieced together, it is time to consider it as poetry.

Hnaef's speech, which begins the fragment, is rich in imagery. The flashing of the Frisian's war-gear is compared to the light of dawn, or a dragon, or a burning hall, images which emphasise the way in which the enemy's torches reflect on their armour – for the attack takes place in the early hours, when it is still dark. The visual imagery is followed by a vivid evocation of the sounds of battle. The bird cries and the howl of the wolf have predatory connotations. These references to "the beasts of battle" are a common convention in Anglo-Saxon poetry, but are deployed to good effect here. Mixed with the noise of the beasts is the noise made by the clashing spears and shields which is emphasised by alliteration on the "g" sound in line 6. This is followed by another evocative image: the moon shining and passing behind the clouds, reminding us that it is still night. Hnaef's final words of encouragement to his warriors are stirring. The description of the thegns preparing for battle emphasises their high status, "goldhladen ðegn" ("gold-adorned thegn", 13) alliterating with "gyrde" ("gird"), their organisation, shown in the rapid way they deploy themselves, their courage – they are "cenum" ("bold", 29) and "deormod" ("daring-hearted", 23), and also considerate, a quality which is shown when Guthere exhorts Garulf, who seems to be a young warrior of high status, not to risk his life in his first experience of battle. The battle that follows is described with vivid imagery, particularly in the line: "banhelm berstan buruhðelu dynede" ("the bone-helms burst, the boards of the burg resounded", 30), the alliteration (which here is onomatopoeic) emphasising the bashing of helmets and the booming of the floorboards. The "reporting" formula "Ne gefrægn ic naefre..." ("I have never heard...", 37) gives the text the authorial stance so common in heroic poetry (for example, *Beowulf*), viz., that of the scop retelling the lore of olden times. In the next few lines the scop takes the opportunity to spell out of one of the principles of the warrior-code (a sort of Bushido for ðegns) in the way that is often done in *Beowulf*: the warriors repaid Hnaef's gift-giving with their courage. "Swetne medo" ("sweet mead", 39) is here a synechdoche for all the gifts a lord would give. Towards the end of the fragment there is more visual description; the dark ravens are contrasted with the "swurdleoma" ("sword-light", 35) that makes the whole of Finnesburh seem on fire, images which link to the beginning of the passage. "Swurdleoma" is one of several kennings which are little flashes of poetry in themselves. Other examples are "guðwudu" ("war-wood", 6) and "sigebeorna" ("victory-warriors", 38).

If the rest of *The Saga of Hengest* was of the same quality, then we have lost a masterpiece which would have been worthy to stand alongside *Beowulf* – possibly the greatest loss of anything in the Anglo-Saxon corpus. *Beowulf*, fine as it is, is a tale of the Nordic homeland, *The Saga of Hengest* would have been a true English National Epic worthy to stand alongside the *Illiad*, the *Aenied*, or the *Nibelungenlied*.

BEOWULF, THE FINN EPISODE

There is only one surviving manuscript of *Beowulf*, known as the Nowell Manuscript after Laurence Nowell, its first owner, though its official title is Cotton Vitellius A.XV. The MS was damaged in the Cotton Library fire at Ashburnham

House in 1731. In 1786 the Icelandic scholar G. J. Thorkelin made two complete copies of the manuscript, one made by himself, the other by a copyist, and returned to Copenhagen to study them. He published the first printed edition of *Beowulf* in 1815. The MS appears to be the working copy of the author. There has been much discussion about the date of the MS with suggestions ranging from the 6th to the 10th centuries. My preference is for a date in the reign of Æthelwulf (839–856) for reasons explained on p. 111, though many other dates have been suggested from the 8th to the early 11th century. The poem refers to events in the early 6th century some of which can be corroborated from literary sources and archaeology. For example, archaeologists in Sweden have excavated the grave mound of Ongenþeow who was buried at some time between 510-515.

...Hnæf Scyldinga,

...Hnaef of the Scyldings,

in Freswæle   feallan scolde. [1070]

in the Frisian slaughter   had to fall.

Ne huru Hildeburh   herian þorfte

Nor did Hildeburh   have need to praise

Eotena treowe;   unsynnum wearð,

the good faith of the Eotens;   she was guiltless,

beloren leofum   æt þam lindplegan,

bereft of her dear ones   in the linden-play,

bearnum ond broðrum;   hie on gebyrd hruron,

her son and brother;   they were born to fall,

gare wunde;   þæt wæs geomuru ides! [1075]

wounded by spears;   that was a mournful woman!

Nalles holinga   Hoces dohtor

Not without reason did   Hoc's daughter

meotodsceaft bemearn,   syþðan morgen com,
grieve over Fate's decree,   when the morning came,

ða heo under swegle   geseon meahte
then she under the sky   could see

morþorbealo maga,   þær heo ær mæste heold
her murdered kinsmen,   where before she had held the most

worolde wynne.   Wig ealle fornam [1080]
joy in the world.   War took all

Finnes þegnas,   nemne feaum anum,
of Finn's thegns,   except a few alone,

þæt he ne mehte   on þæm meðelstede
so that he could not   in that meeting-place

wig Hengeste   wiht gefeohtan,
the battle with Hengest   conclude at all,

ne þa wealafe   wige forþringan
nor the woeful remnant   by battle dislodge

þeodnes ðegne;   ac hig him geþingo budon, [1085]
the prince's thegn;   so they offered them terms,

þæt hie him oðer flet   eal gerymdon,
that they for them the other   dwelling would clear,

healle ond heahsetl,   þæt hie healfre geweald
hall and high settle,   that they would half of it control

wið Eotena bearn,   agan moston,
with the Eotens' sons,   might have,

ond æt feohgyftum,   Folcwaldan sunu
and at the giving of treasure,   Folcwalda's son

dogra gehwylce   Dene weorþode, [1090]
each day   the Danes would honour,

Hengestes heap   hringum wenede,

Hengest's company would   revere with rings,

efne swa swiðe   sincgestreonum

with even as much   precious possessions

fættan goldes,   swa he Fresena cyn

of ornate gold,   exactly as he the Frisian kin

on beorsele   byldan wolde.

in the beer-hall   would embolden.

Ða hie getruwedon   on twa healfa [1095]

Then they pledged   on both sides

fæste frioðuwære.   Fin Hengeste

a firm compact of peace.   Finn to Hengest

elne, unflitme   aðum benemde

with great earnestness   took an oath

þæt he þa wealafe,   weotena dome,

that he the woeful remnant,   by wise men's judgement,

arum heolde,   þæt ðær ænig mon

would hold in honour,   that there any man

wordum ne worcum   wære ne bræce, [1100]

by word nor by deed   would not break the treaty,

ne þurh inwitsearo   æfre gemænden,

nor in malice   ever complain,

ðeah hie hira beaggyfan   banan folgedon,

though they their ring-giver's   killer followed,

ðeodenlease,   þa him swa geþearfod wæs;

leaderless,   and were thus forced by necessity;

gyf þonne Frysna hwylc   frecnan spræce

if then any Frisian   by provocative speech

ðæs morþorhetes   myndgiend wære, [1105]
of the murderous feud   were to remind them,
þonne hit sweordes ecg   seðan scolde.
then it by sword's edge   must be thereafter.
Ad wæs geæfned,   ond icge gold,
The funeral fire was prepared,   and rich gold,
ahæfen of horde.   Herescyldinga
raised from the hoard.   The War-Scyldings'
beadorinca   wæs on bæl gearu.
best warrior   was ready on the bier.
Æt þæm ade wæs   eþgesyne [1110]
At the funeral-pyre was   easily seen
swatfah syrce,   swyn ealgylden,
the blood-stained mail-shirt,   the swine all-golden,
eofer irenheard,   æþeling manig
the boar hard as iron,   the many noblemen
wundum awyrded,   sume on wæle crungon.
destroyed by wounds,   who had fallen in slaughter.
Het ða Hildeburh   æt Hnæfes ade
Then Hildeburh ordered   at Hnaef's pyre
hire selfre sunu   sweoloðe befæstan, [1115]
her own son   committed to the fire,
banfatu bærnan   ond on bæl don
the bone-cases burned,   and put on the bale-fire
eame on eaxle.   Ides gnornode,
beside them both.   The lady lamented,
geomrode giddum.   Guðrinc astah.
sorrowed with songs.   The warrior was laid out.

Wand to wolcnum   wælfyra mæst,
Wound to the clouds   the greatest death-fire,
hlynode for hlawe;   hafelan multon, [1120]
roared before the mound;   heads melted,
bengeato burston,   ðonne blod ætspranc,
the wound-gates burst,   then blood sprang out
laðbite lices.   Lig ealle forswealg,
from the hate-bites of the bodies.   The blaze swallowed all,
gæsta gifrost,   þara ðe þær guð fornam
the greediest guest,   those who there were taken by battle
bega folces;   wæs hira blæd scacen.
from both folk;   their glory was gone.
Gewiton him ða wigend   wica neosian, [1125]
The warriors returned then   to seek their houses,
freondum befeallen,   Frysland geseon,
bereft of friends,   to see Frisia,
hamas ond heaburh.   Hengest ða gyt
their homes and high fort.   Yet Hengest
wælfagne winter   wunode mid Finne,
the battle-stained winter   lived with Finn,
eal unhlitme.   Eard gemunde,
in an unfriendly place.   He remembered his land,
þeah þe he ne meahte   on mere drifan [1130]
though he could not   drive on the sea
hringedstefnan;   holm storme weol,
the ring-prowed ship;   the sea heaved in storm,
won wið winde,   winter yþe beleac
fought against the wind;   the winter locked the waves

84

isgebinde,   oþðæt oþer com
in icy bonds,   until came another

gear in geardas,   swa nu gyt deð,
year to the courtyards,   as it still does now,

þa ðe syngales   sele bewitiað, [1135]
those which continuously   carry out their seasons,

wuldortorhtan weder.   Ða wæs winter scacen,
gloriously bright weather.   Then winter was gone,

fæger foldan bearm.   Fundode wrecca,
the lush fields fair.   The exile departed,

gist of geardum;   he to gyrnwræce
the guest from the court;   he of vengeance

swiðor þohte   þonne to sælade,
sooner thought   than of sea-path,

gif he torngemot   þurhteon mihte [1140]
and whether he a bitter encounter   could bring about

þæt he Eotena bearn   inne gemunde.
that the Eotens' sons   inwardly remembered.

Swa he ne forwyrnde   woroldrædenne,
So he did not refuse   the worldly custom,

þonne him Hunlafing   hildeleoman,
when to him Hunlafing   Battle-light,

billa selest,   on bearm dyde;
the finest blade   he placed on his lap;

þæs wæron mid Eotenum   ecge cuðe. [1145]
among the Eotens   its edges were known.

Swylce ferhðfrecan.   Fin eft begeat
So too his mortal enemies.   Finn in turn received

sweordbealo sliðen æt his selfes ham,

dire sword-onslaught in his own home,

siþðan grimne gripe Guðlaf ond Oslaf,

when concerning the fierce attack Guthlaf and Oslaf,

æfter sæsiðe, sorge, mændon,

following their sea-journey, declared their grief,

ætwiton weana dæl; ne meahte wæfre mod [1150]

blamed for their share of woes; he could not his restless spirit

forhabban in hreþre; ða wæs heal roden

contain in his breast; then the hall was reddened

feonda feorum, swilce Fin slægen,

with the foes' lives, so too Finn was slain,

cyning on corþre, ond seo cwen numen.

the king amid his troop, and the queen was seized.

Sceotend Scyldinga to scypon feredon

Scylding shooters ferried to the ships

eal ingesteald eorðcyninges, [1155]

all of the house-goods of the nation's king,

swylce hie æt Finnes ham findan meahton:

which they at Finn's estate could find:

sigla, searogimma. Hie on sælade

shining jewels and well-cut gems. They on the sea-path

drihtlice wif to Denum feredon,

the noble wife ferried to the Danes,

læddon to leodum. Leoð wæs asungen,

led to the people. The lay was sung,

gleomannes gyd. Gamen eft astah... [1160]

the gleeman's tale. Joy again sprang up...

By a lucky coincidence this episode in *Beowulf* takes up the story of the fight at Finnesburh not long after the *Fragment* leaves off. This lay ("leoð"), as the poet calls it, is sung by the scop at the feast celebrating Beowulf's victory over Grendel. In the lay, Hengest kills Finn in revenge for the attack which led to the killing of prince Hnaef and others, but this context of feud and revenge contains a hint for the main plot of *Beowulf* that the feud will go on, and someone will come seeking revenge. This, of course, comes true all too soon in the shape of Grendel's mother. Since this is a digression from the main plot, and since the hint about coming revenge is the poet's main purpose, it is not surprising that he summarises some parts of the story, for example, the reasons why Hengest decided to break the treaty and take revenge on Finn. However, sections of the passage are narrated with the same vivid detail that we have observed in *The Finnesburh Fragment*. The best example of this is the funeral scene. In this scene, the poet gives us a series of phrases which juxtapose the glamour of the materiel of war with the bloody outcome:

swatfah syrce, swyn ealgylden,
the blood-stained mail-shirt, the swine all-golden,
eofer irenheard, æþeling manig
the boar hard as iron, the many noblemen
wundum awyrded; sume on wæle crungon.
destroyed by wounds; no few had fallen in slaughter.
—*Beowulf,* 1111–1113

The passage ends with a powerful example of Anglo-Saxon understatement, made all the more powerful by the description that precedes it. This is followed by a moving description of Hildeburh's suffering as she watches the bodies of both her son and brother burn. The horror of their death and Hildeburh's grief is emphasised by the detailed description of the way the bodies burn: "...hafelan multon/bengeato burston, ðonne blod ætspranc..." ("heads melted, the wound-gates burst, then blood sprang out...",

1120–1121) emphasised by the alliteration on "bengeato burston" and "blod" and by the vivid kenning in the phrase "laðbite lices" ("from the hate-bites of the bodies", 1122) which reminds us of the horror and futility of the feud which took their lives and which will no doubt take more lives. This futility is emphasised by the phrase "wæs hira blæd scacen" ("their glory was gone", 1124).

After the description of the funeral, the scop quickly summarises the events leading to the killing of Finn and Hengest's return home with Hildeburh and the booty of Finnesburh, though here and there are flashes of vivid poetry which hint at what we have lost in the full version, for example, the vivid description of the icy winter that keeps Hengest imprisoned at Finnesburh:

> ...holm storme weol,
> *...the sea heaved in storm,*
> won wið winde,   winter yþe beleac
> *fought against the wind;   the winter locked the waves*
> isgebinde...
> *in icy bonds...*
> —*Beowulf,* 1131–1133

Finally, with a master touch, the poet returns us to Heorot with a complete change of mood,

> ...Leoð wæs asungen,
> *...The lay was sung,*
> gleomannes gyd.   Gamen eft astah...
> *the gleeman's tale.   Joy again sprang up...*
> —*Beowulf,* 1159–1160

This reminds us that the episode is a digression. Though perhaps "digression" is not the right word, as the Hengest episode is far from irrelevant, hinting as it does of revenge at a key moment in the narrative. As such it adds richness and perspective to the main plot – the genius of the *Beowulf* poet.

LAYAMON'S BRUT

There are two extant copies of the manuscript of Layamon's *Brut*; one in the MS. *Cotton Caligula* A ix, dating from the first quarter of the 13th century, and in the *Cotton Otho* C xiii, copied about fifty years later. It was composed around 1190 (see page xi). As the bulk of my reconstruction is based on this text, three extracts are given: 1. Rowena and Vortimer; 2. Merlin's Mother; 3. Hengest's Fight with Aldolf. Line numbers reference the whole of Layamon's *Brut* (Madden edition, 1847).

1. ROWENA AND VORTIMER

Hit ilomp an are tide   heo nom hire to ræde

It happened at a time   that she took counsel

þat heo wolde fare   to þan kinge Vortimer

that she would go   to king Vortimer

to don bi his ræde   alle hire neode, [7450]

to carry out his advice   which was all she needed,

and to woche time heo mihte wel don vnderuongen þene
   Cristindom.

at which time she might do well   and convert to
   Christendom.

Forð heo gon riden   to Uortimer þan kinge,

Forth she went riding   to Vortimer the king,

þa heo hine imette   uæire heo hine igrette:

fair was their meeting,   fair was their greeting:

"Hal wrð þu lauerd king,   Bruttene deorling!

"Hail to you lord king,   Britain's darling!

Ich æm þe icomen to   Cristindom ich wulle auon [7455]

I have come to you to   become a Christian.

an þan ilke dæie   þe þu seolf demest."

on whatever day   you yourself deem fit."

Þa wæs Uortimer þe king   bliþe þurh alle þing,

Then was Vortimer the king   blithe in everything,

he wende þat hit weore soð   þat þeo scaðe sæide.

he believed it was the truth   what the traitor said.

Bemen þer bleowen,   blisse wes on hirede.

Trumpets were blown,   bliss was in the court.

Forð mon brohte þat water   bi-foren þan kinge. [7460]

Men brought water   before the king.

Heo seten to borde   mid muchelure blisse.

They sat down at the board   with much bliss.

Þa þe king hafde iæten   þa eoden þeines-men to mete;

When the king had eaten   the thegnmen went to eat;

in halle heo drunken,   harpen þer dremden.

in the hall they drank,   the harp delighted.

Þa swicfulle Rouuenne   eode to are tunne

The treacherous Rowena   went to a room

þer wes idon in   þes kinges deoreste win. [7465]

in which she could find   the king's best wine.

Nom heo an honde   ane bolle of ræde golde

She took in her hand   a bowl of red gold

& heo gon scenchen   on þas kinges benche.

and she began serve it   on the king's bench.

Þa heo isæh hire time   heo fulde hir scale of wine

When she saw her time   she filled her cup with wine

& at-foren al þan dringe   heo eode to þan kinge

and before all the warriors   she went to the king

& þus hailede him on   þe swic-fulle wimman. [7470]
and hailed him thus   this treacherous woman.

Lauerd king wæs hail   Uor þe ich am swiðe uæin.
"Lord king, wassail   I am happy for you."

Hercne nu muchel swikedom   of þere luðere wimmon;
Listen now to the great wickedness   of this treacherous woman;

hu heo gon swiken þer   þene king Uortimer!
how she began to betray   king Vortimer!

Þe king heo uæire under-uæng   to his fæie-siðe!
The king received her fair   to his evil fate!

Fortimer spæc Bruttisc   & Rouuenne Saxisc. [7475]
Vortimer spoke British   and Rowena Saxish.

Þan king þuhte gomen inoh   for hire spæche he loh.
The king it was a game   and he laughed at her speech.

Hærcne hu heo toc on   þis swicfulle wimman.
Listen how she took on   this treacherous woman!

In hire bñosme heo bar   bi-neoðen hire titten
In her bosom she bore   beneath her breasts

ane guldene ampulle   of attere i-fulled
a golden ampule   filled with poison

& þa luðere Rouuenne   dronc þene bolle [7480]
and the deceitful Rowena   drained the bowl

þat heo hafde half don   after þes kinges dom,
until she had half done   to the king's doom,

þa while þe þa king loh   þa ampulle heo ut droh,
and while the king laughed   she drew out the ampule,

þene bolle heo sette to hire chin þat atter heo halde in þat win
she put the bowl to her chin   and poured poison in the wine

& seoðen heo þa cuppe   bitahte þan kinge.
and afterwards she gave the cup   to the king.

Þe king dronc al þat win   & þat atter þer-in. [7485]
The king drank all that wine   and the poison therein.

Þe dæi forð eode,   blisse wes on hirede,
The day passed by,   bliss was in the court,

for Uortimer þe gode king   of þan swikedom nuste na-þing,
for Vortimer the good king   of that treachery knew nothing,

for he isah Rouuenne   halden þene bolle,
for he saw Rowena   holding the bowl,

& drinken half þat ilke win   þat heo heuede idon þer-in.
and drinking half of the same wine   that she had put in.

Þa hit com to þare nihte   þa to-dælleden hired-cnihtes,
When it got dark   and the courtiers departed,

& þa ufele Rouwenne   wende to hire inne,
and the evil Rowena   went to her room,

& alle hire cnihtes   mid hire uorð-rihtes,
and every knight   of her guard forthright,

þa heihte heo hire sweines   & ec þaie þeines
then she ordered her swains   and also her thegns

þat heo an hiȝinge   heore hors sculden sadelien
that they with haste   their horses should saddle

& heo swiðe stille   stelen ut of buruwe, [7495]
and they should silently   steal out of the burh,

& wenden al bi nihte   to Þwoncchestre uorð-rihte,
and travel by night   to Thongchester forthright,

& þer swiðe vaste   bi-clusen heom in ane castle,
and make themselves fast   enclosed in a castle,

& luʒen Uortigerne   þat his sune hine wolde biliggen.

and say to Vortigern   that his son would besiege him.

& Vortigerne þe swikele king   ilæfde þare læsing.

And Vortigern the false king   believed the falsehood.

Nu vnder-ʒat Uortimer his sune þat he hefde atter inomen,

Now Vortimer his son   realised that he had taken poison,

ne mihte na lechecraft   helpen him næ wiht.

and that no medical skill   could help him one whit.

He nom feole sonden   & sende ʒeond his londe

He took many messengers   to send over his land

& hehte alle his cnihtes   to him comen forð-rihtes.

and tell all his knights   to come to him forthright.

Þa þat folc was icumen   þa wes þe king swiðe untrumed.

When the folk had arrived   the king barely lived.

Þa ʒirnde þe king heore grið   & þus he spac hem alle wið:

He asked for their peace   and thus he spoke with them all:

"Alre cnihten wrð eow best   þe heren æie kinge.

"Of all knights you are the best   that serve any king.

Þer nis nan oðer red   buten hiʒend-liche ich beo dæd.

No other fate lies ahead   but soon I shall be dead.

Hir ich bitæche eow mi lond   al mi seoluer & al mi gold,

Here I give you my land   all my silver and all my gold,

& alle mine maðmes,   eowre monscipe is þa mare.

and all my wealth,   your worship is the greater.

& ʒe forð-rihtes senden after cnihtes [7510]

And now forthright   send for knights

& ʒeuen heom soluer & gold   & hældeð ʒe seolf eowre lond,

and give them silver and gold   and hold the land yourselves,

& wrekeð eow ȝif ȝe cunnen   of Sexisce monnen,

and wreak revenge if you can   on every Saxon man,

uor weonne so ich beo uorð-faren Hengest eow wul makien kare

for when I am gone from here   Hengest will bring care,

& nimeð mine likamæ   & leggeð an chæsten,

so take my body   and lay it in a chest

& ledeð me to þare sæ-stronde   þer Saxisce men wulleð
    cumen a lond. [7515]

and lead me to the sea-strand   where the Saxons will
    come on land.

Anan swa heo me þer witen   awæi heo wulleð wenden;

As soon as they know   away they will go;

nouðer quic ne dead   ne durren heo me abiden!"

neither alive nor dead   dare they face me!"

I-mong þissen dome   dæd i-warð þe gode king.

In the middle of this command   the good king died.

Þer wes wop þer wes rop   & reuliche iberen.

There was weeping, there was regret   and rueful cries.

Heo nomen þes kinges licame   & ladden to Lundene [7520]

They took the king's body   and brought it to London

& bisides Bælȝes-ȝate   fæire hine bi-burȝeden,

and beside Belyns-gate   buried him honourably,

& nawiht hine ne ladden   alse þe king heihte.

but not at the coast   as the king had ordered.

Þus liuede Uortimer   & þus he endede þar.

Thus lived Vortimer   and thus he ended there.

When reading the *Brut*, we are immediately caught up in the narrative flow, which is relentlessly linear, unlike the ellipital syntax of the Anglo-Saxon texts in which a statement is often made, then repeated in another way, elaborated, or reflected on. For example, in the *Beowulf* Episode, when Hunlaf's son puts a sword in Hengest's lap, the narrative pauses to describe the sword, moves on, then adds more description:

> þonne him Hunlafing   hildeleoman,
> *when to him Hunlafing   battle-light,*
> billa selest,   on bearm dyde;
> *the finest blade,   he placed on his lap;*
> þæs wæron mid Eotenum   ecge cuðe.
> *among the Eotens   its edges were known.*
> —*Beowulf,* 1143–1145

The same is true of the structure of the narrative which is far from being in chronological order. For example, Beowulf's childhood is not described until near the end of the poem (2425ff). The sentence and metrical structure of the *Brut* are much simpler than in *Beowulf*. A quick glance at the text is enough to notice that many lines begin with an ampersand and are end-stopped. Also, there is far less specialised poetic diction. Indeed, the range of vocabulary is relatively small. We also notice that the metre is different to the metre of classical Anglo-Saxon poetry. The first two half-lines are linked by both alliteration and rhyme, yet many lines have neither rhyme nor alliteration, or alliteration only in one half-line Also, the metre is much looser, and not unlike the freer alliterative verse of that acknowledged masterpiece, *Sir Gawain and the Green Knight* (which, for example, has five stressed syllables in the first line). Layamon also varies the number of stressed syllables from line to line, giving an effect which is more like prose in places. These limitations have led some critics to propose that it was written to be read aloud to a mainly illiterate, provincial, non-aristocratic, audience (see Allen, *The Implied*

Audience of Layamon's Brut 1994). However, Layamon makes excellent use of his limited resources. His sentence structure is appropriate for his linear narrative, and his flexible metre avoids the stilted effect that mars much verse chronicle writing – for example Robert Mannyng's version of this story in his *Chronicle* (c. 1338), which in some places is little better than doggerel.

Where Layamon excels is in the compelling narration of a scene and in the writing of dialogue. After setting the scene in the above passage, Layamon creates dramatic tension by contrasting the unsuspecting happiness of Vortimer with the the intended treachery of Rowena:

> Þa wæs Uortimer þe king   bliþe þurh alle þing,
> *Then was Vortimer the king   blithe in everything,*
> he wende þat hit weore soð   þat þeo scaðe sæide.
> *he believed it was the truth   what the traitor said.*
> —*Brut*, 7457–7458

The first line uses rhyme to link the two half-lines together; the second uses alliteration on "s" which emphasises the word "scaðe", a word from Old Norse which means "one who works harm" and which derives from the goddess Scaði (the goddess of revenge).

The phrase "Bruttene deorling!" ("Britain's darling", 7454) in Rowena's greeting reminds us that Vortimer is a much better king than Vortigern, and emphasises the tragedy that is about to happen, which will rob the country of one of the best rulers it has had for a long time. This is followed by a description of "hall joys" which is strongly reminiscent of Anglo-Saxon poetry, both in content and metre, with its highly effective double alliteration on "h" and "d". (See the note on page 111 which comments on a similar phrase earlier in the poem):

> ...in halle heo drunken,   harpen þer dremden.
> *...in the hall they drank,   the harp delighted.*
> —*Brut*, 7463

Rowena then prepares to carry out the wassail ceremony, but her evil intent and the tragic outcome is suggested by the poet, even before we know what she is going to do, by these words:

Hercne nu muchel swikedom   of þere luðere wimmon;
Listen now to the great wickedness of this treacherous woman;
hu heo gon swiken þer   þene king Uortimer!
how she began to betray   king Vortimer!
Þe king heo uæire under-uæng   to his fæie-siðe!
The king received her fair   to his evil fate!
—*Brut,* 7472–7474

The words "Hercne nu" ("Listen now") draw the reader's attention to the poet's indignant description of Rowena's treachery, and the reference to "fæie" ("fate") adds an Anglo-Saxon note of doom.

The narrative contains a realistic awareness of the communication difficulties between Vortimer and Rowena because of the different languages they spoke. Vortimer's amused reaction is full of dramatic irony. He is besotted with Rowena and finds their language problems funny, but the poet has told us in no uncertain terms that she is planning to do him harm. The dramatic irony is emphasised by the rhyme on "gomen inoh" ("game enough") and "loh" ("laughed"):

Fortimer spæc Bruttisc   & Rouuenne Saxisc.
Vortimer spoke British   and Rowena Saxish.
Þan king þuhte gomen inoh   for hire spæche he loh.
The king thought it was a game   and he laughed at her speech.
—*Brut,* 7475–7476

As the scene comes to its climax, Layamon once again calls for our attention and expresses his indignation with the phrase "Hærcne hu heo toc on..." ("Listen how she took on..."). This is followed by a tantalising description of the poisoning which mixes eroticism with horror; the soft bilabials of the "b"s on "bñosme", "bar" and "bi-neoðen", the beauty of the "guldene ampulle" and the contrast, emphasised by alliteration, with what it contains, "attere" ("poison"):

> Hærcne hu heo toc on þis swicfulle wimman!
> *Listen how she took on this treacherous woman!*
> In hire bñosme heo bar bi-neoðen hire titten
> *In her bosom she bore beneath her breasts*
> ane guldene ampulle of attere i-fulled...
> *a golden ampule filled with poison...*
> —*Brut*, 7477 –7479

Soon after this the poet returns to the "hall-joys": "blisse wes on hirede" ("bliss was in the court", 7486) but now with a tragic irony because Vortimer has already taken the poison but doesn't know it yet. When he realises he is dying, he summons his nobles, but dies before he can finish his final speech. The sorrow at his death is movingly conveyed by the line:

> þer wes wop þer wes rop & reuliche iberen.
> *There was weeping, there was regret and rueful cries.*
> —*Brut*, 7519

This owes much of its poetic effect to the internal rhyme on "wop" and "rop" and the alliteration with "reuliche. We can see in this passage that Layamon's *Brut* is much more than a verse chronicle. His story-telling, though linear, is enhanced by finely judged touches of suspense, dramatic irony and pathos, and is expressed in a verse form which uses alliteration and rhyme, not as a slavishly-followed pattern, but as a flexible medium to emphasise meaning. The *Brut* is usually classified as verse chronicle, but a comparison with most other verse chronicles, Robert Mannyng's, for example, will show that such a classification does it a disservice, as it contains some of the finest poetry in Middle English.

2. MERLIN'S MOTHER

Nu wes Mærlinges moder   wunder mere i-wurðen
Now was Merlin's mother   strangely become
in ane haȝe munstre   munchene ihaded. [7845]
in a high minster   a hooded nun.
Þider iwende Eli,   þe reue of Kair-merðin,
Thither went Eli,   the reve of Caermathen,
& nom him þa lafdie   þer heo læi on munstre
and took him the lady   where she lay in the minster
& uorð him gon ærne   to þan kinge Uortigerne
and hurried forth   to king Vortigern
& muchel folc mid him   & ladden þa nunne & Merlin.
and many folk with him   and led the nun and Merlin.
Sone wes þat word cuð   to Vortigernes kinges muð [7850]
The word was soon made known   to King Vortigern
þat icumen wes Eli   & brohte þa lauedi
that Eli was come   and had brought the lady
& Marling heore sune   wes mid hire þer icumen.
and that her son, Merlin,   had come there with her.
Þa wes an liue   Vortigerne bliðe
Then was   Vortigern blithe in life
& þa læuedi aueng   mid swiðe uæire læten
and received the lady   with looks most fair
& Mærlin he bitahte   goden twælf cnihten [7855]
and Merlin he delivered   to twelve good knights
þa weoren þan kinge holde   & hine witen scolden.
who were faithful to the king   and would guard him.

Þa sæiden þe king Vortiger   wið þa nunne he spilede þer:

Then said Vortigern   with the nun he spoke there:

"Gode læuedi sæi me,   sæl þe scal iwurðe,

"Good lady tell me,   it shall go well with you,

whar weoren þu iboren,   wha streonede þe to bearne?"

where were you born,   who begot you as a child?"

Þæ andswarede þa nunne   & hire fader nemnede: [7860]

Then answered the nun   and named her father:

"Þriddendale þis lond   stod a mines fader hond.

"The third part of all this land   stood in my father's hand.

Of þan londe he wes king,   cuð hit wes wide.

Of the land he was king,   it was widely known.

He wes ihaten Conaan,   cnihtene lauerd."

He was named Conan,   lord of knights."

Þa answarede þe king   swulc heo his cun weore:

Then answered the king   as if she were kin:

"Lauedi sæie þu hit me,   sæl þe scal iwurðen. [7865]

"Lady tell it to me,   it shall go well with you.

Her is Mærlin þi sune,   wha streonede hine?

Here is your son, Merlin,   who begot him?

Who wes him a folke   for fader iholden?"

Who did the people think   was his father?"

Þa heng heo hire hæfued   & heolde touward bræsten.

Then she hung her head   and bent toward her breast.

Bi þan kinge heo sæt ful softe   & ane lutle while þohte.

By the king she sat full softly   and thought a little while.

Vmbe while heo spac   & spilede wið þan kinge: [7870]

After a while she spoke   and said to the king:

King ich þe wulle tellen   for seolcuðe spellen.
"King I will tell you   marvellous stories.
Mi fader Conaan þe king   luuede me þurh alle þing.
My father Conan the king   loved me through all things.
Þa iwarð ich on vestme   wunder ane fæir
Then I became in stature   wondrously fair
þa ich wes an uore   fiftene ȝere.
when I was   fifteen years of age.
Þa wunede ich on bure   on wunsele mine, [7875]
Then I dwelt in a bower   in my mansion,
maidene mid me,   wunder ane uæire,
my maidens with me,   wondrously fair,
þenne ich wæs on bedde iswaued   mid soft mine slepen*
and when I was in bed in slumber   with my soft sleep
þen com biuoren   þa fæireste þing þat wes iboren
then came before me   the fairest thing that was ever born
swulc hit weore a muchel cniht   al of golde idiht.
as if it were a tall knight   arrayed in gold.
Þis ich isæh on sweuene   alche niht on slepe. [7880]
This I saw in a dream   each night in sleep.
Þis þing glad me biuoren   and glitenede on golde.
This thing glided before me   and glistened with gold.
Ofte hit me custe,   ofte hit me clupte,
Often it kissed me,   often it embraced me,
ofte hit me to-bæh   & eode me swiðe neh.
often it approached me   and came very near to me.
Þa ich an ænde me bisæh   selcuð me þuhte þas.
When at length I saw myself   this seemed strange to me.

Mi mæte me wes læð,   mine limes uncuðe. [7885]

My flesh was loathsome,   my limbs unusual.

Selcuð me þuhte   what hit beon mihte.

It seemed strange to me   what it might be.

Þa anȝæt ich on ænde   þat ich was mid childe.

Then in the end I perceived   that I was with child.

Þa mi time com   þisne cnaue ich hæfuede.

When my time came   I had this boy.

Nat ic on folde   what his fader weoren,

I know not in this world   who his father was,

ne wha hine biȝate   inne weorlde-riche, [7890]

nor who begot him   in this world's realm,

no whaðer hit weore unwiht   þe on Godes halue idiht.

nor whether it were an evil thing   on God's behalf ordained.

La swa ich ibedde are   nat ich na-mare

Alas as I pray for mercy   I don't know any more

to suggen þe of mine sune,   hu he to worulde is icume.

what to say to you about my son,   how he came into the world.

Þe nunne beh hire hæfde adun   & hire huȝe dihte.

The nun bowed down her head   and covered her features.

The Merlin section of the *Brut* clearly has Celtic origins. Its setting is Wales, and the main character, Merlin, was probably based on Myrddin Wylit, a figure in medieval Welsh legend whom Geoffrey of Monmouth used to elaborate the story of Ambrosius in Nennius' *Historia*. Geoffrey's version was developed by Wace, and later by Layamon. Nennius' account is essentially the same as the later versions, though much shorter. The following extract describes how Ambrosius (Merlin) was discovered, and gives us brief information about his mother which the three later writers, Geoffrey, Wace and Layamon embroidered:

> In consequence of this reply, the king sent messengers throughout Britain, in search of a child born without a father. After having inquired in all the provinces, they came to the field of Ælecti, in the district of Glevesing, where a party of boys were playing at ball. And two of them quarrelling, one said to the other, "O boy without a father, no good will ever happen to you." Upon this, the messengers diligently inquired of the mother and the other boys, whether he had had a father, which his mother denied, saying, "In what manner he was conceived I know not, for I have never had intercourse with any man;" and then she solemnly affirmed that he had no mortal father.

The similarity of this story with the Christian story of the Virgin Birth would not have escaped Christians, nor the implied parallel between Ambrosius/Merlin and Christ. This would have been slightly shocking because Merlin is clearly a pagan figure, similar to Vortigern's wise men and druids, albeit a benevolent one.

The Christian parallel is another feature which is Celtic rather than Anglo-Saxon. Thus, at this point of the Hengest section of the *Brut*, we are furthest away from the putative *Saga of Hengest*. However, the material is too rich to omit. Not only is it fine literature in its own right, but it is important to set the story of Hengest in context as the precursor of the Arthurian age.

As for the passsage's literary qualities, we have already had a brief glimpse of these in the Introduction in which a part of Glowka's critical appreciation was quoted (see page xvii). It is given here in full where the specific references to the original text can be fully appreciated. The "first line" he refers to is line 7877 of the above text. It is also marked with an asterisk.

The first line uses alliterating "s"s as onomatopoetic reminders of sleep (presenting the nun's predilection for labials: *wæs, bedde, iswæued, mid, mine, slepen*). The second line uses rhyme to link half-lines (*biuoren, iboren*), but there is also a possible alliterative link between *biuoren* and *fæireste*; there is also a string of labials. The third line gives a concrete description of the *þing* as a *cniht* who was *idiht* in gold. The last four lines, which I have scanned as having six beats apiece, summarize the repeated nightly visits of the golden knight in rhyming or assonating half-lines of three beats each. However, the first three lines also present the technical achievements of alliterative links: *isæh / sweuene / slepe, glad / glitenede / gold,* and *custe / clupte.* The balanced rhythms, the frequent use of rhyme and assonance, and the surprises of alliteration give the seduction scene preciousness and intensity. The nun, chaste in habit and manner, nevertheless provides an almost titillating description of her experience with the incubus, a description made so by the poetic technique. My impression is that the nun's intensity argues itself as a kind of apology: any maiden would have succumbed to the beautiful golden vision. Layamon's work here rises to the glories of Keats in *The Eve of St. Agnes.*
—A. W. Glowka, *The Poetics of Layamon's Brut* (1994) 61.

It is difficult to compare the literary quality of Layamon's version with Monmouth's or Wace's without being equally familiar with Early Middle English, Latin and Norman-French. However, at the simplest level, the English translation of Monmouth's version is 166 words, Wace's is 190 words, and Layamon's is 240 words, so there is certainly more descriptive detail, which seems to be more poetically expressed, and while it may not quite rise "to the glories of Keats", it is nevertheless a fine passage of poetry.

3. HENGEST'S FIGHT WITH ALDOLF

I þan fæhte com þe eorl,   Aldolf of Gloucetre,
In the fight came the Earl,   Aldolf of Gloucester,
& ifunde Hengest,   cnihten for-cuððest,
and found Hengest,   of knights the wickedest,
whar he feond-liche faht   & þa Cristine feolde.
where he fiendishly fought,   felling Christians.
Aldolf his gode sweord adroh   & uppen Hengest sloh. [8335]
Aldolf drew his good sword   and at Hengest struck.
& Hengest warp þene sceld biuoren & ælles weoren his lif forloren
Hengest had to lift his shield   or lose his life,
& Aldolf smat i þene sceld   þat he atwa to-scænde.
but Aldolf smote the shield   and it split in two,
& Hengest him leop toswulc hit a liun weore,
Then Hengest leapt at him,   like a lion he was,
& smat an Aldolfes helm   þat he atwa to-feol.
and smote Aldolf's helm   so that it split in half.
Þa heowen heo mid sweorde   þa swipen weoren grimme.
They hewed each other with swords   the swipes were grim.
fur flæh of stele   ofte & wel ilome.
Fire flew from steel   often and brightly.
Vnder are stunde,   þa leop Aldolf to grunde,
After a while,   Aldolf fell to the ground,
& isæh him Gorlois,   þat wæs a kene gume ful iwis;
but he saw Gorlois,   who was a brave warrior;
of Cornwale he wes eorl;   he wes widene cuð.
he was the Earl of Cornwall   and widely renowned.

Þa wes þæ beorn Aldolf   muchele þe balder [8345]

Then was the warrior Aldolf   much the bolder

& hæf hæhȝe his sweord   & lette hit adun swippen

and heaved high his sword   and let it swipe down

& smat Hengest a þan hond   þat he forlette his brond,

and smote Hengest on the hand,   so that he dropped his brand,

an hiȝinge hine igrap,   mid grimme his læchen,

and quickly gripped him,   with his grim looks,

bi þere burne hode   þa wes an his hafde

by the byrnie hood   that was on his head

& mid muchelere strengðe   hine adun swipte, [8350]

and with great strength   struck him down,

and seoððe he hine up bræid swulc he hine to-breken wolde,

then brought him up   as though he would break him,

& mid ærmen hine bisprædde,   & forð hine lædde.

and with arms locked around him,   led him away.

Nu wes Hengest inumen   þurh Aldolf þene æhte gume!

Now was Hengest beaten   by Aldolf, brave man!

Þæ cleopede Aldolf,   þene eorl of Gloucestre:

Then cried Aldolf,   the earl of Goucester:

"Hengest nis þe noht swa murie   swa þe wes bi
    Ambresburie, [8355]

*"Hengest, it is no so merry   as it was in
    Ambresbury,*

þer þu þa sæxes droȝen   and Bruttes of-sloȝen.

where you drew your sæxes   and slew the Britons.

Wid muchele swike-dome   þu mi cun sloȝe.

With much treachery   you slew my kindred.

106

Nu þu scalt læn leosen   & losie þine freonden,

Now you shall pay for it   and part with your friends,

mid reoliche witen,   an worlde for-wurðen!"

with fearsome death,   forsake the world!"

Hengest eode stille   ne isæh he help nenne. [8360]

Hengest's was still,   for he saw no help.

Aldolf hine ladde   to his leod-kinge

Aldolf led him   to his folk-king

& grætte þene leod-king   mid leofliche worden:

and greeted the folk-king   with fair words:

"Hail seo þu Aurilien,   aðeles cunnes,

"All hail, Aurelius,   noble ætheling,

her ich bringe þe biuoren   þe wes þines cunnes bone."

here I bring before you   the bane of your kindred."

From the outset the reader is invited to identify with Aldolf. We are reminded that Hengest is "cnihten for-cuððest" ("the wickedest of knights", 8333) and told that he is "Cristine feolde" ("felling Christians", 8334). Layamon has always seen Hengest as the invader, and what is worse, a heathen. That he describes him so positively in the early part of the Hengest section (he is called "cnihtene alre fæirest", "fairest of knights", six times before his epithet changes after the massacre at Ambresbury) may be attributable to his sources and the popular reputation of Hengest as the founding father of the English nation. Here, however, he is definitely the villain.

This raises the question of Layamon's perspective on his material. It is clear that he is broadly pro-English and anti-British from these lines at the end of the *Brut*:

& Ænglisce kinges   walden þas londes
And English kings   ruled this country

& Bruttes hit loseden   þis lond and þas leoden,
and the Britons lost it   this land and this nation,
þat næuere seoððen mære   kinges neoren here.
so that they were never   kings here again.
Þa ȝet ne com þæs ilke dæi beo heonne-uorð alse hit mæi.
It may happen again one day   be it henceforth as it may.
i-wurðe þet iwurðe,   i-wurðe Godes wille.
What will be will be,   may it be God's will!
Amen. [16096]

However, it is probable that his concept of the English is of the newly-emerging nation consisting of the later, Christian Anglo-Saxons, the Normans, and those centrally-based Celts who lived under English rule. Despite this, he identifies with King Arthur to such an extent that he seems to forget that he is the leader of the British resistance to the Saxon occupation, seeing him rather as a Christian champion fighting against the heathen. So far does he forget Arthur's Britishness, that he even writes after his fall: "þat an Arður sculde ȝete cum Anglen to fulste" ("Arthur will come again to help the English", 14295-7).

If Layamon seems somewhat confused about national identity we can hardly blame him, for it is a problem that exists to this day – especially for the "Anglen".

The literary qualities of this passage are comparable with some of the fight scenes in *Beowulf*, hence the epigaph (see below, page 129). The description of the single combat is a blow-by-blow account of what happened. The sheer force and fury of the fight is powerfully communicated by the poet in lines such as:

Þa heowen heo mid sweorde þa swipen weoren grimme.
They hewed each other with swords   the swipes were grim.
—*Brut*, 8340

Also, by details such as Hengest's split shield and Aldolf's split helmet. The description is reinforced by the poet's imagery: Hengest is like a lion ("swulc hit a liun weore", 8338) and the clashing swords making flashes of fire ("fur flæh of stele", 8341). This is followed by a moment of suspense as our hero (remember, Layamon is on Aldolf's side) falls to the ground. But he is helped (or inspired by) Gorlois to renew the fight. More specific details follow. Aldolf strikes Hengest on the hand so that he drops his sword, grabs him by his mail coif, strikes him down, then gets him in an arm-lock. There is an effective touch of description as the poet gives us a glimpse of the expression on Hengest's face: "mid grimme his læchen" ("with his grim looks", 8348). Aldolf's speech to Hengest reminds us that this is a just revenge for Hengest's treachery at Ambresbury. The sheer fury of Aldolf, which helped him to win this close-fought fight, is a result of his desire to revenge his friends. He is thus Hengest's Nemesis, or "scaðe", to use the equivalent English term (see pages 46 and 64). Aldolf describes Hengest's imminent death in a phrase reminiscent of Anglo-Saxon battle poetry: "...& losie þine freonden" ("...and lose your friends", 8358). For a similar expression, "freondum befeallen" ("deprived of friends") see *Beowulf*, 1126, above.

This passage is similar in length, style and descriptive detail to the single combat of Wulf Wonreding with Ongentheow in *Beowulf* (see note on page 129 for more comparisons). However, Wulf's single combat is a digression to illustrate the theme of feuding, whereas Hengest's is one of the main events in the climax of the poem. Thus a comparison with one of Beowulf's monster fights would be more appropriate, even the shortest of which (the fight with Grendel) runs to 150 lines. As Marie-Françoise Alamichel comments:

> Ce tempo beaucoup plus lent de *Beowulf* se manifeste également dans la présentation beaucoup plus riche, plus profonde, plus fine des personnages et de leurs motivations.
> —Alamichel, Marie-Françoise, *Beowulf et le Brut de Lawamon* (1993) p. 10.

The slower pace gives *Beowulf* a richer and deeper presentation of characters and their motivations, and the digressions enrich the narrative with additional layers of meaning. The *Brut,* by comparison, has a rapid narrative pace, and is linear in structure, with the result that it lacks *Beowulf's* depth of significance. However, as the above example shows, it can match *Beowulf's* descriptive poetry on the surface level at least.

Notes

INTRODUCTION

1. Wilson, R. M., *The Lost Literature of Medieval England*. New York (1952) p. 266.
2. Aurner, Nellie Slayton, *Hengest: a Study in Early English Hero Legend*. Iowa (1873) p. 7.
3. Morris, J. *The Age of Arthur*. London (1973) pp. 266-267.
4. The genealogy of Æthelwulf given by Æthelweard and *The Anglo-Saxon Chronicle* goes back (by various routes) to Beo, Scyld and Scef. This remarkable concordance with the genealogy of the kings of the Danes in the opening lines of *Beowulf* suggests that the poem was composed at some time in his reign (839–856).
5. Tolkien, J. R. R., *Finn and Hengest* reprinted in Alan Bliss (ed.), *Finn and Hengest: The Fragment and the Episode*. London (1982) p. 67.
6. Wikipedia, *Hengest and Horsa*, accessed 30/11/12.
7. Radice, Betty (ed.), Geoffrey of Monmouth, *The History of the Kings of Britain*. Harmondsworth (1966) p. 14.
8. Radice, Betty ibid. (1966) p. 191.
9. Radice, Betty ibid. (1966) p. 193.
10. Le Saux, Françoise Hazel Marie, *Layamon's Brut: the poem and its sources*. Cambridge (1989) p. 190.
11. Magoun, F. P., *The Oral-Formulaic Character of Anglo-Saxon Narrative Poetry*. Cambridge, MA. (1953) pp. 446-67.
12. Andersson, Theodore M. *Die Oral-Formulaic Poetry im Germanischen*, in *Heldensage und Heldendichtung im Germanischen*, (ed.) by Heinrich Beck (1988) pp. 1-14.

13. Crowne, D. K., *The Hero on the Beach: An Example of Composition by Theme in Anglo-Saxon Poetry*, in *Neuphilologische Mitteilungen*, 61 (1960) p. 371.
14. Tolkien, J. R. R., *The Monsters and the Critics.* London (1937) p. 19.
15. Chambers, R. W., quoted in J. R. R. Tolkien, ibid. (1937) p. 11.
16. Glowka, Arthur Wayne, *The Poetics of Layamon's Brut*, in Le Saux, Françoise Hazel Marie (ed) *The Text and tradition of Layamon's Brut.* Cambridge (1994) p. 61.
17. See Chickering, Howell D., Jr. (tr.) *Beowulf.* New York (1977), Introduction.
18. See Glowka, Arthur Wayne, *The Poetics of Layamon's Brut* in Le Saux, Françoise Hazel Marie (ed.) ibid. (1994).

BOOK 1, SCYLD

1. The epigraph is taken from *Beowulf* lines 1 – 11: "Listen! We have heard..." The first section of my reconstruction closely follows the opening of *Beowulf* as this is the only example of the beginning of an Anglo-Saxon saga poem that has survived. However, there are many other examples in other types of poem of the opening "Whæt!" ("Listen!") – a call for the audience's attention, e.g., *Exodus* and *Elene*.
2. *Anglecynn* – the Old English name for the Anglo-Saxon peoples.
3. *Scedeland* – the Northern Lands. The word is taken from *Beowulf*, line 19.
4. *Scyld and Scef* – the founders of the Danish dynasty, who for political reasons were also adopted as the founders of the House of Wessex in the reign of Æthelwulf (see note 4 on page 111).
5. *Beaw, Dan and Angul* – I have taken these characters from the *Gesta Danorum*, ch. 1 to explain the common ancestry of the Geats, Danes and Angles which is necessary to my narrative.
6. *Angeln* – a region of modern Schleswig-Holstein, part of

which is still called Angeln today.

7. *Godwulf the Great* – the genealogical information in this section is taken from Nennius' *Historia Brittonum,* ch. 31 expanded with information from the *Gesta Danorum,* ch. 4. Nennius' genealogy includes Wecta, and we know from the *Gesta Danorum* that he was Wærmund's brother. Wærmund was king of Angeln and the father of the famous King Offa I of Angeln. Wecta, according to Nennius, was Hengest's great grandfather, and his grandfather, Witta was a contemporary of Offa. Of course, these genealogies were made to order. Every petty princeling in the Anglo-Saxon period could ask his scop to give him a genealogy stretching back to Woden or Scyld, and thus authenticate his claim to power. There is a good example of this in *The Anglo-Saxon Chronicle* (see note 4 on p 111): Æthelwulf's genealogy was probably constructed to empasises the Danish connection at a time when the Danes were powerful in England. But whatever the historical reality of Hengest's antecedents, Nennius' genealogy and the additional information from the *Gesta Danorum*, show that it was widely believed that Hengest was a member of the royal family of Angeln, and thus well fitted to be the ruler of a new kingdom in Brittania, whether that kingdom was as limited as Kent, or included all the Angle settlements.

8. *Offa* – I have added Wærmund and Offa to Hengest's genealogy on the authority of Saxo Grammaticus. Without the information that Wærmund was Wecta's brother, it is easy to miss the royal connection. Equally important is the connection with Offa. Offa is famous for a single combat with Sueno to settle the argument about a disputed boundary with the Myrgings. That single combat took place in the living memory of Hengest's time, and must have been an inspiration to all Angles. The full story is told by Saxo in the *Gesta Danorum*, and he probably found it in a saga or heroic poem which has since been lost. A reconstruction of part of that lost saga can be found in my book, *Hrothgar*, ISBN 978-1475029048.

9. *Witangemot* – literally, "the meeting of wise men".
10. *"I am exiled from Angeln..."* – the next 20 lines are closely based on the Anglo-Saxon lyric poem *The Wanderer*.

BOOK 2, FINN

1. The epigraph is taken from *The Finnesburh Fragment*. It is translated on page 9 with the line beginning "So wake up now, my warriors!"
2. *Heremod* – mentioned twice in *Beowulf* as an example of a bad king.
3. *a warning from Hnæf* – after this point the text is my translation of *The Finnesburh Fragment*, slightly shortened and simplified. See pp. 73-77 for the original text with a literal interlinear translation.
4. *Sisar* – I have changed the name from Guthlaf to avoid confusion with the Guthlaf in Hengest's band. I chose the same Sisar to link this passage to my reconstruction of Part 1.
5. *The Half-Danes' hero, Hnæf of the Scyldings...* Half-Danes and Scyldings are probably family or clan names of the dominant clans in Denmark at the time. See Tolkien's discussion of this in Alan Bliss (ed.) *Finn and Hengest: The Fragment and the Episode* (1982) 37-50. This raises the issue of Hengest's nationality. If he is an Angle (as stated in later sources), why is he fighting alongside the Danes? The explanation could be that Hengest is an Angle, but is an exile (he is described as a "wrecca", "adventurer" or "exile", in *Beowulf*, 1137) who becomes one of Hnæf's thegns: "þeodnes ðegne" (*Beowulf*, 1085). Tolkien discusses this point in his Glossary of Names (see *Finn and Hengest: The Fragment and the Episode* (1982), 63-76).

   After two and a half lines of linking material my account continues with a shortened version of the Hengest episode in *Beowulf* (lines 1071–1159) which continues the story of the Frisian feud.
6. *linden-play* – a kenning for battle. A "linden" is a synonym for shield as they were often made of linden, a

light, springy, close-grained wood that does not split easily, and is thus a suitable wood for a shield.

7. *Battle-Flame* – my translation of "hilde-leoman" in *Beowulf*, line 1143. This could be a kenning for sword or a proper name. Since important swords are usually named in *Beowulf*, I tend towards the latter interpretation.

8. *Grendel's mother* – I couldn't resist popping in this allusion. *Beowulf* is about monsters, with history in the digressions; *Hengest* is about history, with monsters in the digressions, e.g., the Merlin and the dragons episode. See pp. 57-59 and Introduction page ix.

9. *But cowardly King Hoc* – this is my interpretation of how Hengest came to Britain, based on information from Nennius, who tells us that he was exiled (see introduction pages v to vi).

10. *for three-hundred years...* This prophecy is reported by Gildas (see *De Excidio* ch. 23), and is probably about right, as around three-hundred years later, in 793, a Viking raid on Lindisfarne marked the beginning of the Viking Age which almost destroyed Anglo-Saxon England.

11. *Time passed quickly...* this final section of Book 1, which describes Hengest's journey and landing in Britain, is adapted from *Beowulf*, lines 210–319. It is probable that the oral poets of the Anglo-Saxon period recycled material with a similar subject matter such as funerals, sea-journeys and battles. See Andersson (1988), Crowne (1960), and the discussion in the Introduction, pages xiv to xv.

12. *Pictish raiders* – the Picts were Celtic tribes who lived in eastern and northern Scotland from before the Roman conquest of Britain until the 10th century when they merged with the Gaels.

BOOK 3, VORTIGERN

1. The epigraph is in the Latin of Gildas (*De Excidio et Conquestu Britanniae*, ch. 23, written c. 540), which can be translated as follows:

> At that time all members of the assembly, along with the arrogant usurper Vortigern, are blinded; such is the protection they find for their country (it was, in fact, its destruction) that those wild Saxons, of accursed name, hated by God and men, should be admitted into the island, like wolves into folds, in order to repel the northern nations.

2. *The news came quickly*... from this point to the end of the poem (except the last 14 lines) the text is my translation of the Hengest section of Layamon's *Brut*, lines 6880–8346, with a few minor changes and additions (which are annotated).

3. *war-keels* – in the Latin of Gildas, "cyulis" (ibid. ch 23). This appears to be a translation into Latin of the Anglo-Saxon "ceól" – an Anglo-Saxon synechdoche for ship. It is remarkable that Layamon uses the same synechdoche so many generations later, and he did not copy it from his main source, Wace, who uses the Norman-French word: "navees".

4. *But he failed to tell them*... I added this line to link this passage with the Finnesburh material.

5. *Our gods are good*... this is a surprisingly accurate account of the Anglo-Saxon gods bearing in mind that the *Brut* was written by a Christian priest six centuries after the English were converted to Christianity. It is important to note that he did not get this information from Wace, who only mentions "Woden" and "Frea", using classical names for the other gods. The table below compares Layamon's nomenclature with that of the Anglo-Saxons. It will be noted that several Roman gods are listed. Some of the other gods overlap their Nordic counterparts, such as Woden and Jupiter, and some, like Mercury, have a unique role. It is interesting to speculate whether this accurate knowledge of the Anglo-Saxon gods arises from scholarly research by Layamon, information from English peasants in his pastoral care, or copying from a source other than Wace.

GODS ACCORDING TO LAYAMON

LAYAMON'S BRUT	ANGLO-SAXON	DESCRIPTION/COMMENT
Phebus	Sigel	Sun god
Saturnus	—	The only Roman god after whom a day is named
Woden	Wōden	Chief god
Iupiter	—	Chief god in the Roman pantheon
Mercurius	—	Roman messenger god.
Appollin	—	Unknown, perhaps another version of the sun god
Teruagant	Tīw?	Possibly Termagant, A Middle-Eastern war god
Fræ æ	Frēo	Goddess of love, beauty and fertility
Þunre	Þunor	God of thunder
Monen	Mōn	Moon god
Tidea	Tīw?	God of single combat, victory and heroism

6. *Then came the Picts, painted and horrible...* This and the following 21 lines were written by me incorporating Layamon with some additional description inspired by Hall's *Old English Idyls* (see below). This is how it read before my poetic flight of fancy:

> The Picts were come on this side of the Humber,
> and King Vortigern of their coming was well aware.
> Together they came and many were slain.
> There was very fierce fighting, very stern combat.
> The Picts were used to vanquishing Vortigern
> and they thought to do it again, but it turned out differently,
> for it was a great help that Hengest was there,
> and the strong knights who came from Saxland
> and the brave Germans who came with Horsa,

for very many Picts they slew in the fight.
Fiendishly they fought, the fated fell!
When noon was come the Picts were overcome
and quickly they fled on each side of the Forth,
all day they ran an unreckonable number.

This is the passage from Hall (pp. 7-8) that inspired my attempt to embellish Layamon's description. It conveys well the sheer horror of the Pictish raids, and helps us to understand why Vortigern would go to any lengths to put an end to them:

The brave-hearted, battle-true barons of Saxony,
Will lend us their aid, our land and dear ones
To defend from the furious, fiery, implacable
Fiends of the north. Foemen oppress us,
Cruelly harry us, killing and slaying us;
Men of the Picts painted and horrible,
Those grim, grisly and ghastly destroyers,
From the north swooping are sacking and burning
Our hedges and homesteads, heedless of pity...

7. *the fated fell...* I kept this line from Layamon. It is a translation of "feollen þa fæie" which is almost identical to "faege feollon" in *The Battle of Brunanburh*, line 12.
8. *They drank, they dreamed, delight was theirs!* – The line recalls several descriptions of "hall-joys" in Anglo-Saxon poetry where an earlier version of Layamon's "dremden" (here translated as "dreamed") is used ("dreomen" – to revel).
9. *ground his shears...* Layamon's text uses the word "sæxes" which suggests the craftsman was using the single-edged Saxon short sword rather than shears as we know them today.
10. *by confusion of letters...* the capital letter thorn (Þ) can be mistaken for a "D" by those who are not familiar with it. "Þong-chastre" is identified by Layamon as Lancaster, but I think Doncaster is more likely as that area was the

base of Hengest's operations against the Picts. A similar story to the Þong-chastre story is told about York and the Viking Ivar the Boneless.

11. *Caer Conan* – modern Conisbrough. This and the next eight lines were written by me to emphasise the Conisbrough connection which is made clear later in Layamon's poem.

12. *a fortress* – there is evidence that an Ancient British hill fort stood on the site of Conisbrough Castle. If Hengest really did go there, he would probably have found one of the forts that had been refortified after the Roman legions left. Whatever it was, he didn't think it strong enough to hold out against Aurelius. The present castle was begun by Hamelin Plantagenet in about 1180, though many earlier historians believed it to be an example of early Saxon work from the days of the Heptarchy (see, for example, the note to Ch. XLI in the 1798 edition of Ivanhoe by Sir Walter Scott) and some even believed it to be built by Hengest himself.

BOOK 4, ROWENA

1. The epigraph is from *Beowulf*, lines 1162 – 1172:

> ...Wealhtheow came forth
> glistening in gold to greet the good pair,
> uncle and nephew; their new peace held
> each true to the other. Likewise Unferth,
> spokesman at court, sat at Hrothgar's feet:
> all his kinsmen knew he had courage,
> except when edges met. Then Wealhtheow spoke:
> "Accept this cup, my noble lord,
> gold-giving king, be joyful and generous,
> a treasure-friend to all..."

It describes a similar welcome ceremony to the one in which Rowena takes the welcome cup to king Vortigern, thus confirming the authenticity of the description given by Layamon (and his antecedents Geoffrey and Wace). The above description begins immediately after the "scop" (court poet) has finished his lay about Hengest and the Frisian feud, and continues for a further 59 lines in which Wealhtheow takes the welcome cup to her sons, Hrethric and Hrothmund, and then to Beowulf. She also gives him gifts of two arm bands, a mail shirt, rings, and a large gold torque (collar).

2. *Rowena* – the early sources do not give the name of Hengest's daughter. Its first appearance is in Geoffrey's *Historia*. However, possible confirmation of the name appears in the Welsh *Triads*, the earliest manuscript of which dates from the 14th century, but which records earlier bardic material:

TRIAD 37

Three Fortunate Concealments
of the Island of Britain

The Head of Bran the Blessed, son of Llyr, which was concealed in the White Hill in London, with its face towards France. And as long as it was in the position in which it was put there, no Saxon Oppression would ever come to this Island; The second Fortunate Concealment: the Dragons in Dinas Emrys, which llud son of Beli concealed; And the third: the Bones of Gwerthefyr the Blessed, in the Chief Ports of this Island. And as long as they remained in that concealment, no Saxon Oppression would ever come to this Island. And there were the Three Unfortunate Disclosures when these were disclosed. And Gwrtheyrn the Thin disclosed the bones of Gwerthefyr the Blessed from the love of a woman: that was Ronnwen the pagan woman; and it was he who disclosed the Dragons; and

Arthur disclosed the head of Bran the Blessed from the White Hill because it did not seem right to him that this Island should be defended by the strength of anyone but by his own.

Geoffrey of Monmouth spells her name "Renwein" which is similar to the Welsh spelling. Layamon spells her name "Rouwenne" (the final syllable was probably pronounced) and sometimes "Rouwen" when the metre needs two syllables. It is possible that the name was derived from the Anglo-Saxon "Hrothwynn", meaning "fame and joy". The name was later modernised to "Rowena", probably by Sir Walter Scott who uses the name for a beautiful Saxon lady in his novel, *Ivanhoe* (1819). It is probable that he found the name in Geoffrey's *Historia*.

There is very little description of her in Geoffrey's *Historia*, or Layamon's *Brut*. However, Wace, in his *Roman de Brut*, gives this brief description:

Now the maiden was gracious of body, and passing fair of face, dainty and tall, and shapely of person. She stood before the king in a web of fine raiment, and ravished his eyes beyond measure.

As there is only a brief reference to an unnamed daughter of Hengest in the earliest source to mention her (Nennius), this description is undoubtedly an example of Wace's creative elaboration of Monmouth's *Historia*.

As for her age, she must have been very young, as her father could not have been much older than 30 at the time of the Finnesburh incident, or he would have been too old to fight in that last battle in 488. This date is given in *The Anglo-Saxon Chronicle* as the date that his son assumed the kingship of Kent, and thus implies Hengest's death. Assuming Hengest married at an early age, Rowena would have been about 15 at the time of the Finnesburh incident, and perhaps 16 when she married Vortigern. Girls were married much earlier in the medieval period, for example, Richard II's marriage to Isabel of France, aged 6. Of course, Rowena would need to be old enough to exude the sexual attraction that lured Vortigern against his better judgement.

Later chroniclers, e.g., Roger of Wendover (d. 1236), describe a pregnant Rowena being imprisoned in the Tower of London after the British rebellion against Vortigern in 464. The anachronistic reference to the Tower of London (built 1078) is an indication of how seriously we should take that piece of information. The same is probably true of stories that she poisoned Aurelius after he became king, and later Uther. It is the kind of trick she could only get away with once!

3. *a golden-haired girl* – this, the next four lines, and the two lines beginning "and they clung to her body..." on page 27, were written by me because a description of Rowena is lacking in the *Brut*. I was inspired by Lesslie Hall's *Old English Idyls* (1899), which contains a most wonderful description of Rowena which I wish I had written myself. At the risk of eclipsing everything I have written in this book, I give the following extract from his description:

> Sweetest to Hengist
> Of all that had come o'er the cup of the billows,
> O'er the mingling of waters, westward and southward
> Was the lady Rowena, the lovely, beautiful,
> Gem-brilliant maiden, jewel and darling
> Of Hengist the hero: the harp and the gleeman
> Have sung for ages the elf-bright folk-maiden's
> Beauty and loveliness. Broad her renown is;
> Forever and ever England shall honor her
> As first of her fair-haired, fond-loved myriads
> Of beautiful maidens, mothers and daughters
> And sisters of heroes: the sweet-toned harp,

Joy-wood beloved, long shall continue
To sing her glory in saga and story,
Lovely, illustrious lady Rowena,
Leading the line of beloved, winsome
Women of England, elf-brightest, purest
Of mothers and maidens that men ever sought for
Or earls ever fought for.

4. *wassail* – from Anglo-Saxon "wæs hal" ("be in good health"), a common greeting, (for example, *Beowulf*, line 407: "Wæs þu, Hroðgar, hal!"). It is also used as a toast, or as a word for a drinking bout, and it is in this sense that it is preserved in many Christmas carols, some of them of ancient origin. For example, here is the first verse of *The Gloucestershire Wassail*:

Wassail! Wassail! all over the town,
Our toast it is white and our ale it is brown;
Our bowl it is made of the white maple tree;
With the wassailing bowl, we'll drink to thee.

See also Hamlet's speech in *Hamlet*, Act 1, Scene 4:

The king doth wake to-night and takes his rouse,
Keeps wassail, and the swaggering up-spring reels;
And, as he drains his draughts of Rhenish down,
The kettle-drum and trumpet thus bray out
The triumph of his pledge.

5. *Sevira* – Vortigern's wife (sometimes spelled "Severa") Eliseg's Pillar is the only source naming Vortigern's wife. Eliseg's Pillar is the remaining portion of a tall round-shafted cross of Mercian type. All that survives today is part of the rounded lower shaft, on one side of which it is just possible to see weathered traces of early lettering. Fortunately, a detailed record of the original inscription was made in 1696 by the antiquarian Edward Lhuyd:

Maximus of Britain [Conce]nn, Pascen[t], Mau[n], An[n]an [+] Britu, moreover, (was) the son of Guorthi(girn), whom Germanus blessed and whom Severa bore to him, the daughter of Maximus the king, who slew the king of the Romans +

Layamon does not mention the name of Vortigern's wife, so I inserted it here for the sake of completeness. From this passage it appears that Vortigern was only nominally a Christian. He had another wife or wives under Celtic law, and had no compunction about taking yet another (Rowena) under Anglo-Saxon heathen law. It seems to be the heathenness rather than the polygamy that upsets the Britons.

6. *Ardora* – the name of Vortigern's daughter is not mentioned in any of the early sources and may well be a later invention. See also note 16 on page 125.

7. *Octa* – *The Anglo-Saxon Chronicle* gives the name of Hengest's son as Æsc, sometimes spelled Oisc. He became king of Kent and was succeeded by an Octa, so there is clearly some confusion in the early sources. This is discussed at length by Tolkien in his essay *Finn and Hengest* (pp. 75-76).

8. *twelve pennies* – an anachronism. The penny was introduced by King Offa, king of Mercia, in 757.

9. *Epiford* – possibly Aylesford in Kent.

10. *Derwent* – there are four River Derwents in Britain. The ones in Derbyshire or Yorkshire are the most likely.

11. *Katiger met Horsa in single combat* – this single combat is given only a brief mention by Layamon, so I have added a few lines of description, once again inspired by Lesslie-Hall's *Old English Idyls*, from which the following is an extract:

> The hot-mooded, fire-breathing
> Horsa and Catigern clashed in the battle,
> Lashing and slashing with sword-blades that rattled;

> Fierce was their fury. Fire, then, glimmered,
> Sword-sparks bright brilliantly shimmered;
> Felaláf's eye flashed his wrath, then,
> Brave-hearted battle-sword. Bitterly fought the two
> High-hearted heros; I have never heard of
> Earls angrier, eagerer to grapple
> Each other in battle...

12. *Thanet* – the Isle of Thanet lays at the most easterly point of Kent. While in the past it was separated from the mainland by the nearly 2000 feet-wide River Wantsum, it is no longer an island

13. *Pope Romain* – the pope at the time of Germain's visit was actually Pope Celestine I (422 until April 6, 432).

14. *Germain of Auxerre and Louis of Troyes* – see introduction pages vi-vii.

15. *Pelagius* – Pelagius (c. 354–c. 420/440) was an ascetic who denied the doctrine of original sin as developed by Augustine of Hippo, and was declared a heretic by the Council of Carthage in 418. His interpretation of the doctrine of free will became known as Pelagianism.

16. *Ardora* – This incident is not included by Layamon, but since it helps to build up the picture of Vortigern's depravity I decided to included it. My source is Nennius' *Historia Brittonum*, ch. 39:

> In the meantime, Vortigern, as if desirous of adding to the evils he had already occasioned, married his own daughter, by whom he had a son. When this was made known to St. Germanus, he came, with all the British clergy, to reprove him: and whilst a numerous assembly of the ecclesiastics and laity were in consultation, the weak king ordered his daughter to appear before them, and in the presence of all to present her son to St. Germanus, and declare that he was the father of the child. The immodest woman obeyed; and St. Germanus, taking the child, said, "I will be

a father to you, my son; nor will I dismiss you till a razor, scissors, and comb, are given to me, and it is allowed you to give them to your carnal father." The child obeyed St. Germanus, and, going to his father Vortigern, said to him, "Thou art my father; shave and cut the hair of my head." The king blushed, and was silent; and, without replying to the child, arose in great anger, and fled from the presence of St. Germanus, execrated and condemned by the whole synod.

In chapter 48, Nennius tell us what happened to Ardora's son:

The fourth was Faustus, born of an incestuous marriage with his daughter, who was brought up and educated by St. Germanus. He built a large monastery on the banks of the river Renis, called after his name, and which remains to the present period.

Ardora herself is believed to have ended up in a nunnery.

17. *Guorthegirnaim* – we learn from the genealogy of Vortigern given by Nennius (*Historia Brittonum*, ch. 49) that Guorthegirnaim was an ancient kingdom in Wales, and Vortigern's ancestral inheritance.

18. *Belyns-gate* – probably on the River Thames somewhere near Westminster. A similar story about a burial mound being intended to frighten away enemies appears in *Ragnar Lodbrok's Saga*.

BOOK 5, ALDOLF

1. The epigraph is from Layamon's *Brut*, 7619–7625, which is translated on page 45, beginning with the words: "*Sieze your seaxes...*"

2. *Ambresbury* – Amesbury, a town in Wiltshire near Stonehenge.

3. *The place was Aelenge, now known as Stonehenge* – according to Geoffrey, Stonehenge did not exist on this site at this date but was later brought there from Ireland by Merlin's magic, which made the stones light enough to be easily transported. They were re-erected on the present site to commemorate the massacre of the British noblemen described in this section.

4. *"Nimeð eoure sexes!"* ("Take your seaxes!"). Layamon's Semi-Saxon is here very close to literary West-Saxon, which would be: "Nimað ower sexes!". Compare this with Wace's "Nim eure sexes!" and Monmouth's "Nemet oure saxes!", which is even further from the Anglo-Saxon original. It is interesting to note that Nennius's version, "Nimed eure saxes!" is also close to the original.

5. *Essex* – the origins of many county names can be seen in their spelling. These early tribal groups quickly evolved into the Heptarchy – the seven Anglo-Saxon kingdoms into which England was divided from about 500 to 850. These were Northumbria, Mercia, East Anglia, Essex, Kent, Sussex and Wessex. Of these, Northumbria, East Anglia, Essex and Kent were populated mainly by Angles.

BOOK 6, MERLIN

1. The epigraph represents the Brythonic language spoken throughout Britain in the 5th century. It is an extract from *The Book of Taliesin* (Llyfr Taliesin) which is one of the most famous of Middle Welsh manuscripts. Though the MS dates from the first half of the 14th century much of the content originates in the 10th century. The epigraph is taken from a section entitled, *The Greater Prophecy of Britain*:

> Myrddin (Merlin) tells us how
> An assembly at Aber Peryddon

> Will bring the High King's stewards
> (They will moan of death)
> To gather taxes
> The Cymry (Welsh) will not pay.
> Mary's Mabon, sovereign Word,
> Unbroken by Saxon battery!

It is interesting that the text goes on to mention Hengest and Horsa:

> Down with Gwtheyrn's pariahs!
> Foreign foes will go into exile,
> No welcome anywhere, no land given -
> Rivers will be strange to them everywhere!
> Hengist and Horsa bought Thanet
> With deceit and guile; since then
> They have grown ever stronger.

2. *The Mount of Reir* – Geoffrey calls this Mount Erith and it is widely believed to be Dinas Emrys, which means in Welsh, "The Fortress of Ambrosius". It is a large hillock near Beddgelert in Gwynedd, North-West Wales where there are the remains of a Celtic hill fort which, unusually, had stone walls. The fort pre-dates the Roman invasion, but may have been refortified in the 5th century. It also contains an underground pool which provides another link with the legend – no signs of dragons however!

3. *your mother* – later sources have attributed several different names to Merlin's mother including, Aldan, Joan, Marinia and Optima. Of these, the Celtic Aldan seems the most likely.

4. *Totnes* – a town at the head of the estuary of the River Dart in Devon.

5. *Armorica* – the ancient name for Brittany. The name Brittany, or Little Britain, probably arose from the increasing Brythonic settlement by Britons fleeing from the Anglo-Saxon invasion of the 5th century.

6. *the world then to an end shall come* – don't panic! I slipped this in for a bit of fun on 21/12/12 which was the end of the world according to the Mayan calendar.

BOOK 7, AURELIUS

1. The epigraph is from *Beowulf*, lines 2965 – 2975.

> Wonred's son, the brave Wulf,
> Swung his weapon so that blood spurted
> from his brow, a glancing blow,
> but the old Scylfing was not afraid.
> He quickly struck a stronger blow
> for that bloody blow; a bad exchange
> for the son of Wonred, who staggered back.
> The old man had hit so hard on his helmet
> that, covered all over in a cascade of blood,
> he went down headlong.

This description of a single combat between Wulf Wonreding (a thegn of Hygelac, King of the Geats) and Ongentheow (King of Sweden, of the Scylfing dynasty) is comparable to the single combat between Aldolf and Hengest in Book 7. The description continues for 20 lines and ends with the despondent reflection:

> That is the feud, the fighting of tribes,
> war-lust of men, for which I expect
> the Swedish people will seek us out.

For this episode is one of the digressions in *Beowulf*. The story is told near the end of the poem to show what the Geats can expect from the Swedes now that their protector, Beowulf, has been killed by the dragon. Thus it has the force of an extended metaphor which enriches the texture of the poetry of *Beowulf*, and which is lacking in Layamon's description which is a straightforward narration of a single combat.

2. *Genoure* – probably, Ganarew, a village in south Herefordshire, near the River Wye and the border with Wales. Cloard could be Little Doward in Monmouthshire. There is clearly some confusion in the sources as we have previously been told that Vortigern's stronghold is at Mount Erith (see above).

3. *mount* – Layamon uses the word "munede", and later in the same passage he uses the word "dune". "Bead-es-Dune" is how the Anglo-Saxon version of Bede's *Ecclesiastical History* (c. 10th century) translates "Mons Badonicus" (Mount Badon) in the Latin version. Now "bead" (beado, beadu) means "battle" and "dune" (dún) means "dune" or "hill", so this literally means "Battle of the Dune". In line 8285 of the *Brut*, Hengest is described as "halden ouer dune" ("hurrying over the dune"). Furthermore, the battle that follows puts a decisive end to the first wave of Anglo-Saxon invasion. There is therefore a strong possibility that this could be the famous battle of Mount Badon. This theory is supported by Bede's account in *Ecclesiastical History*, ch. 16, of the events leading up to the battle:

> When the army of the enemy, having destroyed and dispersed the natives, had returned home to their own settlements, the Britons began by degrees to take heart, and gather strength, sallying out of the lurking places where they had concealed themselves, and with one accord imploring the Divine help, that they might not utterly be destroyed. They had at that time for their leader, Ambrosius Aurelianus, a man of worth, who alone, by chance, of the Roman nation had survived the storm, in which his parents, who were of the royal race, had perished. Under him the Britons revived, and offering battle to the victors, by the help of God, gained the victory. From that day, sometimes the natives, and sometimes their enemies, prevailed,

till the year of the siege of Badon-hill, when they made no small slaughter of those enemies, about forty-four years after their arrival in England.

This is remarkably similar to our story so far, but there is no mention of King Arthur. Neither Bede nor Gildas, the earliest sources, mention Arthur, but both are emphatic that it was Aurelius Ambrosius who defeated the Anglo-Saxons. Even the location is more likely than the other candidates for Mount Badon, Bath, or elsewhere in the south-west, as Hengest was more likely to be based somewhere south of the River Humber in order to prosecute his campaign against the Picts. Finally, Bede's estimate of the date of Badon is only five years later than the date of Hengest's death in *The Anglo-Saxon Chronicle* (488).

An alternative theory is that the series of battles described in Monmouth/Layamon which culminate in Hengest final battle, are identical with: "The second, third, fourth, and fifth, [battles] on the Duglas, another river in the land that is called Linuis" described by Nennius in the *Historia Brittonum*. Monmouth states that Vortigern gave Hengest the kingdom of Lindsey. Lindsey, of course is a later Anglo-Saxon kingdom, but its name was derived from the British kingdom of Linnaeus, so it is possible that Nennius is locating some of Arthur's battles in the region around Conisbrough.

But where is King Arthur in Bede's account? In Nennius' *Historia*, Arthur is never called "king". Rather, he is clearly what the Romans called a "dux bellorum" – a man chosen to lead a battle or series of battles: "And though there were many more noble than himself, yet he was twelve times chosen their commander". After these battles, Arthur went north and fought a battle at "Cat Coit Celidon", which is probably the Caldeonian forest in Scotland – no doubt the Picts were on the rampage again. Then it seems that he turned south to the City of the Legions (Chester) to deal with the Saxons who were invading from the south, and perhaps the Scots, from Ireland, and finally Badon (probably Bath) where he fought the decisive battle. This interpretation is consistent with what Gildas tells us of Aurelius. Thus it may be that our "Bead-es-Dune", even if it is not the decisive battle, is one of a series of battles by which the "dux bellorum", Athur, established control of Britain on behalf of King Aurelius Ambrosius.

4. *the Draco banner...* I added these four lines to emphasise the fulfilment of Merlin's prophecy. The Draco banner was like a windsock in the shape of a dragon. The White (or gold) Dragon is the symbol associated with the Anglo-Saxons, and was the symbol of Wessex. A depiction of the Wessex Dragon Banner appears in the Bayeux tapestry. This is the ancient symbol of England rather that the Cross of St George – so maybe we should start flying it at football matches!

5. *by the iron nasal of his Northman's helmet* – this is taken from Geoffrey of Monmouth's version. Layamon writes "bi þere burne hode" (by the hood of his hauberk) which sounds as though he is thinking of the mail coif of his own time.

6. *Agag* – See 1 Samuel, chapter 15, verse 33: "And Samuel said, As thy sword hath made women childless, so shall thy mother be childless among women. And Samuel hewed Agag in pieces before the LORD in Gilgal." This extended Christian reference is in marked contrast to *The Finnesburh Fragment* which is uniquely in the Anglo-Saxon corpus contains no Christian references. Overall, religious references in the *Brut* are handled more consistently than in *Beowulf.* Hengest and his followers are unashamedly Wodenist, and the clash of faiths with Christianity is one of the key sources of tension in the narrative.

7. *barrow-grave* – near to the entrance of Conisbrough Castle is an unusual mound of earth. Tradition says that this is Hengest's barrow. The mound was excavated in or around 1815 but no remains or artifacts were found. A

similar tradition links a tumulus at Horsted in Sussex with Horsa (see Isaac Taylor, *Words and Places: or, Etymological Illustrations of History.* (1865) p. 309).

8. *Cwædon þæt he wære...* these are the last three lines of *Beowulf* (3180 –3182), which I have translated as follows:

> They said that he was, of the world's kings,
> the most generous and the most gentle of men,
> the kindest to his people, and the keenest for fame.

These words, which are Beowulf's epitaph, show him as the ideal Scandinavian lord and warrior; the example to which all others should aspire. Not only is he supremely brave, as shown in his battles with the three monsters, and emphasised by the fact that he chose to face Grendel without weapons, and the dragon by himself, but he is also "mon-þwærust" (kind, gentle, philan-thropic). By using these words as an end-epigraph, I wanted to draw a contrast with Hengest who is an ambivalent figure at best. The revenge he takes at Finnesburh might be excused because he is torn between conflicting loyalties, but it is not so easy to excuse his behaviour on the Night of the Long Knives (see pages 44-47) even if we take into account that he was partly motivated by revenge for his brother. On the other hand, he serves Vortigern loyally until he is driven out by the British rebellion (see pages 29-38) gives land generously to his followers, and finally pays for his treachery in true Aristotelian fashion when Aldolf defeats him in single combat. Hengest's claim to fame, however, is not that he was an exemplary lord and warrior, but that he was the first named Englishman to settle in the country rather than merely raid it. Also, like Beowulf, he was the indispensable protector of his people: Beowulf's death meant the eventual destruction of the Geats, and Hengest's death meant the end of the Anglo-Saxon conquest and occupation of Britain for at least a generation.

BiBLiOGRAPhy

Alamichel, Marie- Françoise, *Beowulf et le Brut de Lawamon*, in *Etudes André Crépin*, 1-10, Buschinger and Spiewok, Geifswald, 1993.

Allen, Rosamund, *The Implied Audience of Layamon's Brut*, in Le Saux, Françoise Hazel Marie (ed.), *The Text and tradition of Layamon's Brut*. Lausanne, Switzerland, 1994.

Andersson, Theodore M. *Die Oral-Formulaic Poetry im Germanischen*, in *Heldensage und Heldendichtung im Germanischen,* (ed.), Heinrich Beck, Berlin, De Gruyter, 1988.

Aurner, Nellie Slayton, *Hengest: a Study in Early English Hero Legend*. Iowa, University of Iowa Humanistic studies, 1873.

Chickering, Howell D., Jr. (trans.), *Beowulf: A Dual-Language Edition*. New York, Anchor Books, 1977.

Crowne, D. K., *The Hero on the Beach: An Example of Composition by Theme in Anglo-Saxon Poetry*, in *Neuphilologische Mitteilungen*, 61. Helsinki, University of Helsinki, 1960.

Garmonsway, G. N. (ed.), *The Anglo-Saxon Chronicle*. New York, Dent, Dutton, 1972.

Hall, John Lesslie, *Old English Idyls*. Boston, Ginn, 1899.

Heaney, Seamus (trans.), *Beowulf: A New Verse Translation*. London, Faber and Faber, 1999.

Le Saux, Françoise Hazel Marie (ed.), *Layamon's Brut: the Poem and its Sources.* Lausanne, Switzerland, 1989.

Le Saux, Françoise Hazel Marie (ed.), *The Text and Tradition of Layamon's Brut.* Lausanne, Switzerland, 1994.

Madden, Sir F., *Layamon's Brut, or Chronicle of Britain; a Poetical Paraphrase of the Brut of Wace.* London, Society of Antiquaries of London, 1847.

Magoun, F. P., *The Oral-Formulaic Character of Anglo-Saxon Narrative Poetry*, in *Speculum*, Vol 28, No. 3. Cambridge, MA, The Medieval Acadamy of America, 1953.

Morris, John, *The Age of Arthur.* London, Wiedenfeld and Nicolson, 1973.

Owen-Crocker, Gale, *The Four Funerals in Beowulf: and the Structure of the Poem*, in *The Review of English Studies*, Vol. 53, Part 209. Oxford, OUP, 2002.

Radice, Betty (ed.). *Geoffrey of Monmouth: The History of the Kings of Britain.* Harmondsworth, Penguin, 1966.

Stenton, Sir Frank M., *Anglo-Saxon England.* Oxford, OUP, 1973.

Taylor, Rev. Isaac, *Words and Places: or, Etymological Illustrations of History.* London and Cambridge, Macmillan, 1865.

Tolkien, J. R. R., *Finn and Hengest,* reprinted in Bliss, Alan (ed.), *Finn and Hengest: The Fragment and the Episode.* London, Allen & Unwin, 1982.

Tolkien, J. R. R., *The Monsters and the Critics.* London, Allen & Unwin, 1937.

Wilson, R. M., *The Lost Literature of Medieval England.* London, Methuen, 1952.

Wright, C. E. *The Cultivation of Saga in Anglo-Saxon England*, Edinburgh, Oliver and Boyd, 1939.

About the Author

In Conisbrough, in the West Riding, I spent most of my childhood where there's an old castle presiding over the local neighbourhood. The castle teased me with its mystery and got me interested in history. Later, I went to Lampeter, studying the English Language there. I liked Old Norse and Anglo-Saxon, the sagas and the poetry, the culture and the history – and now I show appreciation by trying my hand at translation.

www.ingramcontent.com/pod-product-compliance
Lightning Source LLC
Chambersburg PA
CBHW020308150626
46552CB00022B/2086